IS SALVATION REALLY FREE?

IS SALVATION REALLY FREE?

EDWARD W.H. VICK

Review and Herald Publishing Association
Washington, DC 20039-0555
Hagerstown, MD 21740

This book was
Edited by Richard W. Coffen
Designed by Howard Bullard

PRINTED IN U.S.A.

Library of Congress Cataloging in Publication Data

Vick, Edward W. H.
Is salvation really free?

1. Salvation. 2. Faith. I. Title.
BT751.2.V53 1983 234 82-25014
ISBN 0-8280-0152-9

CONTENTS

A Preliminary Word to the Reader

Throughout the years I have held certain clear convictions. Here is one: If the believer and the church give the central matters their rightful position of first importance, other concerns will fall into place and receive the consideration that they in turn deserve. Take, for instance, the matter of doctrine. If we do not see what the really important and crucial issues are, we run the risk of devoting undue attention to unimportant issues. People get excited about the peripherals of the Christian message only when they do not discern or when they forget what beliefs and practices are truly essential.

What, then, is the remedy? We must not delude ourselves that there is a final cure-all for the problems of the church. One thing, however, is certain. The church will enjoy spiritual health only when it sees what is really important and emphasizes that. This holds true on all levels—from the gathering of the smallest congregation for nurture from the Word to the largest of gatherings to enact the business of the church, from the theologians as they work out their systems to the students as they pursue their courses and to the preachers as they mount their pulpits.

The preacher must rise to the challenge to put first things first, indeed to perceive what the things are that should be put first. As a preacher I have always been interested in preaching about the important things. There just was only so much time. So I had to use that time to best advantage, for the building up of the waiting congregation. As a result, I have found myself gravitating more and more to the theme represented in this book. It is an old theme, but then our basic questions are as old as humanity itself.

Certain events that transpired in the history of our first century gave a decisive and final answer to that old question "What must I do to be saved?" Not only that, the God who came to us *then* for our redemption is the God who comes to us in our need *now*. He is our contemporary. His hand overflows with gifts. His voice calls for discipleship. He comes to us here and now and asks for our response, not just once and for all, but all the time. However, we cannot fulfill His demand—the demand of a holy and loving God—unless we know the price of discipleship. He freely gives us

His grace, but it is not cheap. It costs us everything.

This, then, is the theme of this book: the love of a gracious God and the faith of responding trust. The chapters seek to give clear expression to themes that spring out of the attempt to understand the love of God as known by faith. I hope that they will, through the grace of God, provide an avenue for clearer understanding and a vehicle for the Spirit of God to make His presence available ever and again.

The book takes a particular form. A brief summary introduces each chapter, and a series of questions concludes each chapter. The questions should assist in the recall and understanding of the themes expounded. These instructional aids will help the reader comprehend what is presented and will aid the memory.

Now a word about the arrangement of the book. First, I set forth in a summary way the meaning of the Christian gospel. God gives all; we receive all (chapter 1). Humanity needs to be given all, and so to receive all, because it is enmeshed in the predicament that sin has brought. The Christian gospel has to do with the plight of the sinner (chapter 2). It tells of what God has done for sinners to relieve them of their burden. Faith has an object. That object is God, who came to the world in Jesus Christ and who went to the cross. The events that have called faith into being have also given it its distinctiveness. Before there is faith, there is the cross and the God who acts through it (chapter 3). The God who comes to us is the God whose providence overrules all. Faith can grasp that providence even when appearances seem to give the lie to the conviction that God is a God of love and worthy of absolute trust. Always behind the frowning providence is the smiling face of a God who loves to the uttermost. Christian faith grasps this truth because faith has had its source in the activity of that God through the death on the cross (chapter 4). The Christian's faith also recognizes God as the Creator. Christian faith is in the One who is ultimate and before whom there was nothing. He who was "in the beginning" is the God whom faith worships (chapter 5).

The next two chapters address themselves to the Reformation conviction that it is by faith alone that God's righteousness is known. In genuine humility, faith receives the gift of forgiveness as sinners accept the acceptance of God (chapters 6 and 7). Whenever one speaks of the faith of the believers as the instrument of their acceptance, it becomes necessary to make clear the nature of discipleship and obedience. Does the law have no place? If it has a place, what is that place? To these questions we next give attention (chapters 8 and 9). After justification what? What is the nature of the holiness to which Christians aspire? What is sanctification? Saints are those who continue to believe that God accepts them. Sanctification is continuance in the acceptance known to faith (chapter 10). But how can I know that it is God in whom I believe? The conviction of the believer is that God is known in faith. This knowledge has to be nurtured. It is nurtured by being expressed and by being fed on faith's former expressions (chapter 11).

What is the nature of faith's reward? Certainly Christians can speak of reward, but how they speak of it is all-important. The Christian reward is the reward of faith, or gift of grace (chapter 12).

Before us continuously opens the choice between two responses to God's activity in Jesus Christ. There is the continuing possibility that God's demand shall offend us. But there is also the possibility of faith when we have gotten past the stumbling (chapter 13).

The final chapter (14) expresses my desire for you, that you may know the life of faith. Given originally as a New Year meditation, it reminds us that every day we may begin anew.

So I bid you, Have faith!

Chapter 1

All Is of Grace, by Faith Alone

The expression "All is of grace, by faith alone" summarizes the Christian gospel. It lays down in a sentence what is essential to the Christian confession.

"All is of grace" means that God's loving will and gracious activity provide everything necessary for the reconciliation of humanity to Him. "By faith alone" means that we must respond in a particular way to what God has provided. Faith is the instrument through which the grace that effects reconciliation comes to us.

Faith—as well as all that has to do with salvation—is of grace. The response appropriate to the giving of grace is the thankful receiving of faith.

Grace, then, is the *source* and faith is the *instrument* of God's saving activity. Reconciliation is *of* grace, *by* faith. The faith that responds to God's grace is itself an effect of that grace. If it is not, it is a human work. Faith does not save us. God saves us. Faith is God's gift, not our work. Faith is not the one work that God accepts in preference to others. Faith is never independent of its source, which is grace—the loving will of God. Faith is *of* grace, and we are reconciled to God *by* faith.

God comes to us in Jesus Christ. Here is where God's grace is manifest. We come to God in Jesus Christ. To this place our faith is directed.

Since faith is of grace and all is of grace, faith is inclusive. Works are exclusive. If we understand faith aright, we cannot say, "Faith *and* works." All is included in grace, which is *by* faith.

The sentence "All is of grace, by faith alone" summarizes the Christian message. Of course, it is very condensed, but it has the advantage that a cartoon has. It calls attention to certain features that must not be missed if we are to understand the point. So our sentence points us to certain essential features of the gospel, and we cannot bypass these if we wish to know the essence of Christianity.

Moreover, it is a Biblical claim. This brief sentence puts the teaching of the Scriptures into a nutshell. Now, when we look at a slogan or a cartoon we must, as we say, read between the lines. It is easy to misunderstand a slogan because we can read between the lines wrongly. We would inevitably misunderstand a cartoon if it portrayed certain things that we did not understand. So with our sentence. It can stand as a résumé of Protestant Christianity only as we understand what the expressions mean and why they are put together in such an apparently paradoxical fashion. For the word *alone* does seem to contradict the word *all*!

Since the expression "All is of grace, by faith alone" is a kind of shorthand for the Christian message, let us summarize the message that it presents. We shall do so by setting forth six points. The Biblical message, the heart of Christianity, that this slogan represents may be expressed in the following propositions:

1. Grace is necessary because sin is destructive.
2. Our salvation (from sin and estrangement) comes from God. He provides it in the man Jesus.
3. Salvation consists in the effecting of a proper relationship between us and God.
4. In this restoration God takes the initiative and *offers* grace to us. Grace is free.
5. "God's grace or mercy is only complete when it is accepted."[1] Faith is the name for that acceptance. There is no reconciliation where there is no faith.
6. Faith has an object, without which it would be empty. Faith is directed to and determined by God, who was revealed in Jesus Christ and who went to the cross and rose again.

All, alone! The two words, at first glance, might seem to imply an antithesis. If all is of grace, how can we speak of "faith alone"? Together or separately the two phrases are a shorthand way of laying bare the heart of the Christian gospel. "All is of grace" stresses the priority of God's loving will. "By faith alone" stresses the necessity of the responsiveness of our will, but to do so in a certain way. God is the source of that reconciliation that we know when we respond in faith to the expression of His grace. We may put it in an ever shorter sentence: God saves that person who has faith in Him.

Now, it is very important how we say this. One false step here can sell out the substance of the Christian gospel. As usual, if we get a few really fundamental matters right, the direction in which we move will also be right. But we can never get peripheral matters right if we go wrong at the center. So we *must* get the central matters correct. A wrong perspective here, be it apparently so slight, will cause distortion of vision everywhere. Our task, then, is to see as clearly as we may at the center. It is a genuinely difficult, but vitally important, task to perform.

For the sake of clarity we cannot spare any word, in the clause that is our subject matter, except the verb. If we left it out we could be no briefer. All of grace, by faith alone. Our task now is to expound carefully the meaning of the clause *as a whole.* We will see that it fitly expresses the Christian message.

Both parts of the clause are necessary. We do not save ourselves. We do not come to know God unaided. We experience the knowledge of God's grace. There is no knowledge of God, of course, that is not experienced. To speak of a knowledge of God, a salvation, that no one had ever experienced would involve a contradiction of terms. But in speaking of experience it is easy to leave the impression that we are talking only of ourselves. Some might assume, then, that our experience of reconciliation terminates in ourselves and has no ground in reality apart from us. The first phrase—All is of grace—guards against this prevalent mistake. Grace means God, and God is not a human being. When we are saved we know that it is none of our doing. Salvation has been given to us. God's acceptance of us is a gift. So in speaking of it we must always put God first. To say *grace* is to say *God.* To preach the gospel of Jesus Christ is to speak of God. The subject matter of the Christian witness is what God has done. That is always primary. In any confession of faith it must always come first. God is the source of all. God's grace is before the human race and precedes our response.

If the error of subjectivism must be avoided at all costs, so also must the fallacy of a false objectivism. That is why the second phrase is so important. The expression "by faith alone" is essential for two reasons.

First, it tells us that God does not save us in spite of ourselves. God does not forgive a person who will not be forgiven. A gift is not given until it is received. "God's active love or grace or mercy is only complete when it is accepted. It is consummated in fellowship, . . . but it is not fully manifested except in 'believers.' 'The love of Jesus, what it is, None but His loved ones know.' "[2] God wills to give, but there must be willing response. We must believe. God's will of grace provides what we must accept.

Second, the act of God is ineffective without a particular kind of response. The response is to be appropriate to the provision. No other will suffice. By faith alone.

It is essential to preserve the order of the phrases. Although faith is essential and although without it there is no reconciliation, the word about grace must come first. The loving will of God is first and foremost. It is primary and prior. It is always *prevenient.* Before we respond, the loving will of God enables us to respond. The life and death of the man Christ Jesus manifested the loving will of God in the most concrete manner possible before we responded. So the word about God's grace must always come first, because God's grace is first. "In the beginning God" (Genesis 1:1).*

The exclusiveness of grace is expressed in the word *all.* There is one source of reconciliation—God. In His gracious provision for and the effecting of reconciliation, He has no rival, for He has no peer. His love is without compare. His will is without equal. His loving will is ultimate. If the redemption of us who are less than ultimate is to be effected, it will be because He who is the Ultimate Reality comes to us in our weakness and need. The alternative is that He may not come. The Christian gospel is that He has come. He has come to us, and that tells us what kind of Ultimate He is. He reveals Himself. He does not wait for the impossible, that is, for us to discover Him. The Christian message springs from a revelation by God, not from human discovery. The God of Christian faith is the God who comes to the human race. He comes because of what He is—love. He loves us who of our own self-wills have deliberately defied Him and set ourselves against Him.

From first to last, all is of grace. Acceptance with God (sometimes called justification) is of grace. We sinners "are justified by his grace as a gift, through the redemption which is in Christ Jesus" (Romans 3:24). Since we are justified by faith and since salvation is of grace, then the faith by which we believe is itself also the gift of God's grace. If we turn to God and experience His grace, it will be because that grace has already been in operation. So the believers are described as "those who through grace had believed" (Acts 18:27). Faith is not a human creation. It is God's gift. "Unto you it is given . . . to believe on him" (Philippians 1:29, K.J.V.).

There is nothing in the reversal of our condition that we do not receive. All is of grace. "For by grace you have been saved through faith; and this is not your own doing, it is the gift of God" (Ephesians 2:8). In the New Testament the decisive and the determining factor in face of our sin is God's grace. Another way of saying this is to insist that salvation is a gift, pure and simple.

If grace is given and its benefits are received, then our appropriate attitude is one of humble acceptance and gratitude.

---

*Unless otherwise noted, all Bible verses are from the Revised Standard Version of the Bible, copyrighted 1946, 1952 © 1971, 1973.

Indeed, the word *grace (charis)* signifies both the good will of the one who makes the gift and the thankfulness of the one who receives it. There can be no thought of being paid for services rendered when what God has given to us through Jesus Christ is a gift, pure and simple. Paul made the antithesis stark and plain: "But if it is by grace, it is no longer on the basis of works, otherwise grace would no longer be grace" (Romans 11:6). Either salvation is free or it is earned. If it is earned, then something other than grace is being spoken of. What is earned is not grace. "Now to one who works, his wages are not reckoned as a gift but as his due" (chapter 4:4).

We now begin to see what grace means. God's grace is Himself. It is His love, called into new expression by human sinfulness. Grace is God's disposition to love us in spite of our sin. It is His love for us in our blind and heedless sinfulness. It is His continuing love despite our persistent willfulness and pride. What God does springs from what He is. God is gracious. If we speak of a transition from sinlessness to sinfulness, grace is the name we give to the new expression of God's love in face of the new and negative reality that has now come to be.

Furthermore, God Himself directs that love toward and not against sinners. For God's love is *agapē,* the selfless love that seeks not its own but is other-directed. Thus God's grace is absolutely free. *Gratia gratuita* was Augustine's dictum: "Grace is free."[3] In the nature of the case it must be. It cannot be bought. If grace, giving, is the Ultimate Reality and if we are estranged from that Ultimate, we must *receive* the gift of acceptance. Receiving is the proper response to giving. Since God is God and there is none other than He (Christians are monotheists) and since His way is to give, then all is given. All has its source here at the Fountainhead of grace. The essential gift contains all. In giving Himself, God has given all. All is of grace.

So we must say *of.* That small preposition points to the source. The Fount of all that is, has been, or will come to be is grace. In the will of a gracious God we find the spring of all. All that has to do with our reconciliation has its source here. There is no source of reconciliation independent of this grace. There is only one Source, God. We are not the source of our salvation in any degree. All is of God. To deny the *all* is to deny everything. To take away a little here is to take away everything. Apart from God there is nothing. Our dependence must be upon God entirely. All is *of* grace. To deny that all is *of* grace is to deny the ultimacy of God.

If all is of grace, the faith that grasps this grace must be included also. Since all is of grace, even the response that we are enabled to make to that grace comes from the effectiveness of that grace. Where grace is effective it shows up in the reality of the believer's faith. The nature of Christian faith is determined by that from which is has its source. Grace is effective through a certain kind of response, the response that its presence makes possible. Grace is the source and faith is the instrument of God's saving activity, which Scripture frequently calls the "righteousness of God."

The very faith by which estranged beings grasp the gift of graciousness is itself an effect of that grace. Only as we say this can we avoid the assumption that faith is a human work. It is not. Faith is *not* the one work that God accepts. We can affirm the uniqueness of faith only as we affirm its dependence. God's grace is prior. The faith by which we believe is dependent.

Through this faith, which grace has enabled, we come to acceptance with God, and also to a knowledge of this acceptance. Grace is the source. Faith is the instrument. The little word *by* emphasizes and never lets us forget that faith does not save us. God saves us. All is of grace. Faith is not an independent reality that God recognizes as the one worthy capacity of man.

Only as we put the emphasis upon the right matter here can we avoid a subjectivistic approach. By laying the stress upon grace as the source of faith and by defining grace as the transcendent, loving will of God, we have already avoided Pelagianism and legalism. We shall see later that as we lay stress upon the holiness and the absolute demand of God, we can avoid antinomianism. Faith is dependent. It is a gift. It is dependent upon God the Ultimate. It is the response to His proffer of acceptance. It is received in the attitude of submission. Reconciliation is *by* faith.

The only way by which we come to the reconciliation God offers us is by faith. Without faith there is no reconciliation. We must never overlook the essential importance of the preposition *by*. Faith is the instrument by means of which we receive the gift. It is not the independent ground for that gift. Faith is never independent. It is always dependent upon its object.

Just as water takes shape from the vessel into which is is poured, so faith takes its shape from that which is its object. Faith is directed toward the gracious God and is determined by Him. Apart from its relation to God, faith has no substance and hence no contours. Faith has saving significance only in relation to Jesus Christ, which relationship, so to speak, makes it what it is.

The faith by which we are reconciled to God is itself *of* grace. So ran the Reformation conviction. The Reformers placed Jesus Christ in the center. Reconciliation was due to his activity. Faith was dependent upon that activity. So John Calvin could write: "Faith of itself does not possess the power of justifying, but only in so far as it receives Christ. . . . We say that, properly speaking, God alone justifies. . . . We compare faith to a kind of vessel; for unless we come empty and with the mouth of our soul open to seek Christ's grace, we are not capable of receiving Christ. . . . In teaching that before His righteousness is received Christ is received in faith, we do not take the power of justifying away from Christ. . . . Faith, which is only the instrument for receiving righteousness, is ignorantly confused with Christ, who is the material cause and at the same time the Author and Minister of this great benefit."[4]

In Jesus Christ, God proffers us a love that is stronger than death, a love expressed in death and victorious over death. He comes to us with His gift of acceptance. He will clear away the ground and open the path to reconciliation. He calls for a response like the response that we make to one whom we love. His deed of love makes that response, difficult as it is, the only appropriate one possible.

When He calls us to take His gift of love, He enables us to respond as faith is born. He is, as it were, on both sides of the relationship that He is attempting to create. So in a most paradoxical way Christians say that God is over against us, and also within us.

Christians are Trinitarian. We cannot avoid it, because we have known the reality of God's grace. We then confess our faith in a certain kind of God. To confess that in the present we have faith in God and that that God is known in Jesus Christ is to confess the doctrine of the Trinity. Only one appropriate response is possible to the gracious God of our Lord Jesus Christ, who comes to us through the Spirit. Only one. The response of faith. God saves us by faith alone. Faith is unique—and unaccompanied.

Faith is alone in that it is unaccompanied by whatever would destroy its very genius. That is really only another way of saying that it is unique. When we say, "By faith alone," we affirm that faith does not need to be accompanied by some work or other to serve as the instrument of God's gracious acceptance. It is all-inclusive.

Whatever is necessary for the effecting and the progressing

continuation of relationship with God is given with faith. So we cannot say, "Faith *and* works." All we need to say is "by faith." Faith is inclusive. Works are exclusive. We are justified by faith alone, that is to say, justified by ("by" means through the instrumentality of), nothing else than, nothing other than, nothing beside, nothing in addition to, faith. Grammatically, "by faith" qualifies "being justified," and "alone" qualifies "by faith." Both are adverbial qualifiers. If we ask the question, "How (by what means) are we justified?" the answer is, "by faith." If we further ask (as Luther did) "and how by faith?" (what does this mean with respect to other activities we perform?), the answer is, "alone," that is to say, "only by faith, by nothing else." By using the adjective *alone,* we cut out as alternatives anything that cannot be comprehended by faith. At the same time we are affirming that everything that is of the essence of salvation can be comprehended by faith.

Thus we avoid antinomianism, the doctrine declaring that when we talk of faith, especially if we say, "By faith alone," we are denying any place for works. When we include works within faith and say, "By faith alone," we are cutting off any kind of dependence upon works of any sort, while stressing that the person of faith performs works of all sorts.

Questions

1. What is meant by the phrase "the priority of God's grace"?
2. Why must the Christian always give grace the first place?
3. Summarize the Christian gospel.
4. What is involved in saying that faith is a gift of God's grace?

Chapter 2

Sin

God forgives sin and accepts the sinner. Sin is rebellion against God, enmity with neighbor, and violation of self. Such sin is manifest at the Fall, and also at the cross. Sin leads to blindness and so is not seen for what it is. Illusions abound. The seriousness of sin is missed. We are led to think that the long passage of time can cancel the sin committed and that sin concerns no one but ourselves. Worst of all, we tend to confuse sin with goodness.

Our rebellion against God is remedied as God, taking the initiative, goes to the cross and reconciles rebels to Himself by offering them pardon, even in their supreme act of rebellion.

Our enmity toward our fellows is remedied as love for God makes possible fellowship between human beings. When we are reconciled to God, hostility to others is removed.

Our violation of ourselves is remedied by forgiveness. To those who can neither forgive themselves nor live with their guilt comes the invitation and promise, "Be forgiven."

To ask in penitence, "God, be merciful to me, a sinner," is to pray a prayer that never goes unanswered.

"O God, have mercy upon us, miserable sinners." We never outgrow the need to offer that prayer, for it describes what we are. It is an admission that we have been helped to see what we are. Since we are all sinners, our entire life should be a prayer for penitence.

" 'God, be merciful to me a sinner!' " (Luke 18:13). That is the cry of penitence. It is also the cry of hope. To pray it in hopeful penitence is to know that God accepts me. I rise from my knees newly forgiven and go down to my house justified.

This is the good news of Christianity. At its heart the Christian gospel says: God forgives sin. We do not have to carry our guilt. In Jesus Christ, God accepts us. Enter into joy! Pass from sorrow's night to the gladness of day! God loves you! After the Fall comes the cross. After sin comes forgiveness—and victory. After the cross comes the resurrection. The good news is both invitation and demand: " 'Come, follow me' " (Mark 10:21).

The gospel deals with the reality of sin. God calls to us in our fallenness. It is we as sinners who are forgiven. We who have shaken our fists in God's face, who have walked with roughshod feet upon our fellows, we who have cleft our own selves in two—we are the rebels whom God forgives.

Sin is rebellion against God. The story of the Fall makes this known. We are assisted in self-assertion, assisted by one who has already gone beyond the barrier to self-assertion and who desires his own self-assertion to be supported by another. When the fruit is plucked from the tree, the will to self-assertiveness has become fact. It is the act of God-forgetfulness. One has forgotten that God is the Creator, that God created the tree.

But sin is also manifest at the cross—what was done against this fellow man was done against God. Since this man was no ordinary person, this act against him cannot be classified with other ordinary acts and dismissed as having equal insignificance. When Friday turned to Saturday that week, a deed had been perpetrated such as had never before been accomplished. Death had intervened between God and humanity.

Sin is enmity with one's neighbor. The story of the Fall clearly reveals this. With the Fall begins the conflict of human being against human being, the opposition and the blaming, and the turning of the other into an instrument for escaping responsibility.

It is also manifest at the cross, where the supreme example of enmity against the fellow man comes into sharpest focus. A good man—whose continual acts of goodness and mercy, sympathy and healing, expressed what goodness means—is thrust out of the way. Wicked, ordinary people cannot stand extraordinary goodness. It must be done to the death—and so it was. In the crucifixion we witness the supreme act of man against his fellow man. For he who was crucified was true and genuine man.

Sin is violation of the self. From the Fall story we learn that temptation means a conscious inducement to veer from known right. It involves selling the self at some deep level of personal being. In this sense all sin is spiritual in that all sin has to do with the twist at the center of personal being.

Such sin is manifest at the cross. If we can truly say that there was a cross in the heart of God before it was planted on Calvary, it is true also of the human heart. The cross was in the human heart before it was set up on Golgotha. It originated in the sin against the self, and man found companions to support him—men like himself. The event of the cross expresses both the love of God and the sinfulness of humanity.

Sin is not a passing phase that we can outgrow. We are what we will. We are what we do. We are what we think. We think of time passing, evening coming, and the sun setting on a different person from the one upon whom it rose. A door opens and closes, and we have entered. It opens and closes again. We enter and we exit and we are never the same again.

This is the nature of the human predicament. Illusions abound, for the very nature of sinfulness leads inevitably to illusion. As a result we call our blurred vision clarity of sight. The disease is devastating, and we call it health. The death that is upon us we call life. We call the illusion that descends upon us insight. Sin blinds, twists, distorts, even the vaunted reason of mankind. Illusions proliferate in our condition of sinfulness. Sin produces the illusion of sin's illusoriness. It is as though the injection that will bring death produces the coma in which we dream of life.

What are some of these illusions?

1. That sin is insignificant: that God is unreal. "He will forgive sin; that is His business," cries the discontented but uncommitted. "I exist for my own sake, and whatever gods there be are subsidiary and unimportant in comparison to my life. If there is such a thing as error or mistake or wrong, that is not very important. I am all-important."

It is a defiance that can be made in subtle ways. To whatever extent God is unreal, to that extent sin is insignificant. For when God is absent, there the individual assumes importance. Just as the noise in the classroom increases in direct proportion to the master's distance from it, so our satisfaction in ourselves increases as God becomes more distant and our understanding of the seriousness of sin decreases.

2. That time cancels sin: that because something was done long ago it has now become less serious. We may even have forgotten. But the God with whom we deal is not temporal but eternal. He is not finite but infinite. But, we say, the past is gone. But the past does not simply disappear with the passage of time. Sin does not diminish or vanish with the passing of the years. It is an illusion to think that it does.

We so easily reconcile ourselves with our past! We like to forget. We speak of the past with tolerance, even with humor. But God lives in an eternal present. For Him the unforgiven sin is always as if it were even now being committed. It is as though we were still in the midst of the argument that was to separate us from our fellows. It is as if we were still relating the story that we have not bothered to understand and that will help ruin the life of another. It is as though we were even now taking the money that does not belong to us. It is as if we were still behind the doors that we had thought had closed upon us forever. No, the passage of time does not remove sin. But the grace of God does. So Scripture says: "'Every one who *believes in him* receives forgiveness of sins through his name'" (Acts 10:43).

3. That sin is my personal affair. But this is simply not true. Whatever we do has its influence. What I do makes a difference, however small, to what I am. And over against what I am stands what I could be. Since I am not a solitary creature, what I am—when I could have been better—influences my relations to others.

Am I mean and unjust? The decision I make may have far-reaching consequences upon someone else, consequences that I cannot predict. But if I rest content to be unjust, I shall not care about those consequences. Am I impure? Then my children's children could suffer seriously. If I am self-centered in my lust, I shall not care about those consequences. But not to care is different from denying that there are consequences. Am I dishonest? Have I cheated someone? Have I neglected my parental responsibility? Who can predict what difference it might have made had I not done so?

If each of us were nearer to what we might have been, how different the world would be! No, sin is not only my personal affair. "None of us lives to himself, and none of us dies to himself" (Romans 14:7).

4. That confuses sin with goodness. It says, "I'm as good as the next person." But one's relationship with God does not depend on one's goodness. Since our relationship with God depends on something other than our goodness, there is no point in pleading our goodness. The highest pinnacle of human goodness, of human justice, of human law-keeping, of human achievement, is still human. And between the human and the divine stretches a great gulf. All that is human stands under the judgment of God. There can be no appeal to that which God has condemned. The confession of faith knows that "we have all become like one who is unclean, and all our righteous deeds are like a polluted garment" (Isaiah 64:6).

The cross has revealed human sinfulness. But it also has revealed the depths of God's love. The same event that shows sin in all its malignity also shows love in its invincibility. Where humanity may do its worst, even there God is present, turning to universal good the petty and restricted hatreds of a few provincial individuals. The cross reveals us in our sin, and it is a sorry picture.

The cross also reveals God in His love, and thus reveals genuine humanity. At the cross we behold man the sinner, God the reconciler, and the true man.

In our sin we have rebelled against God, brought ourselves into enmity with our neighbor, and have violated our very selfhood. But the remedy for the ailment comprehends us as we find ourselves in this threefold condition. In the name of Jesus Christ the Lord, we bring again the good news: There is healing; there is balm; there is restoration.

Humanity's rebellion against God is remedied as God takes the initiative in reconciling mankind to Himself. It is remedied only in this way. The remedy for rebellion is reconciliation. It is God who reconciles. He reconciles mankind to Himself. "We beseech you on behalf of Christ, be reconciled to God" (2 Corinthians 5:20).

But we like to fight. If we have a choice between combat and quiescence, we choose conflict, even if the conflict is a lost cause from the outset. At times the futility of the conflict dawns upon us, but we continue to fight nevertheless. We refuse to lay down our weapons because we enjoy the conflict or because we find fighting the accustomed thing to do and know no other way. At times the futility of the conflict dawns on us, but then we find that our moral wills are not our own to do what we will. So in despair we continue to fight—and to fail.

But we are not alone. The experience is not unique to us. Fighting and failing have marked the history of the race. There was a fall. There is continuous falling.

But after the Fall there is the cross. God has manifested Himself there. There He both moves against the rebels and attracts them to Himself. Jesus prays, " 'Father, forgive them; for they know not . . . ' " (Luke 23:34). The rebels are asked to enter into the fruits of the dying Lord. We are invited to do so. We are also commanded to do so. It is an obligation laid upon us—the acknowledgment of the lordship of Jesus Christ, who provides the forgiveness that issues in reconciliation. We can deny the obligation thus laid upon us, but we cannot escape it. The call to reconciliation is the call to discipleship. It is the all-embracing call, "Follow me."

Man's enmity against his fellow is remedied through a fellowship that love to God alone makes possible. The brotherhood of man does not exist except with the recognition of the fatherhood of God. But we are hostile by nature. We have our precious egos that have to be nurtured, our sensitive feelings that must not be hurt, and our prestige that must be guarded from the competition of others. We are like the wasp that carries the sting in its tail. When everything is all right and the summer air is warm and friendly and no one approaches too near the nest, all is well. But the sting is in the tail—and wasps sting!

When God reconciles humanity to Himself the sting is removed. Genuine and fruitful relations with one's fellow become possible. The fellow is a brother. His or her welfare is to be guarded as much as, in fact, even more than, my own. The other's success is more important than my pride. The initiative, talents, and opportunities I previously used to thwart and destroy genuine relationship with others are now redirected. No longer do I use my neighbor as a steppingstone to my dignity or my success or my reputation. In my awareness of reconciliation with God, the hatred, the contention, the strife, and the jealousy are removed in Jesus Christ.

We are not the first to have acted in such a manner. There was a fall. But after the Fall there was a cross. And from the cross come the words " 'Father, forgive them.' " Calvary manifests the rule of the kingdom of heaven. In the midst of the strife, the jealousy, and the contention are heard the impossible words, " 'Father, forgive them.' " At Golgotha we can see the loving initiative of God in face of the abject rejection by mankind.

Humanity's violation of itself is remedied by forgiveness. We speak the truth when we say, "I shall never forgive myself." We cannot. We cannot live to bear our guilt and we can do nothing about it. That is the nature of the human predicament. The only way to live with the past is to have it forgiven. The only way to live with sin is to live with it as forgiven sin. The only way to *be* a sinner is to be a forgiven sinner. And the only way to be a forgiven sinner is to cast oneself upon God's mercy.

But we are rebels. We are egocentric. We persist in our pride and we will not bend the knee. We will not lift our hands high above the head in surrender. We will not receive the gift. We will strive for self-forgiveness, but we will not yield.

And we have not been the first. This is the way of the world. There was a fall. But after the Fall there is the cross. From without comes the help that we can by no means give ourselves. God freely gives the help, but it demands no less than all, for it is sin that is being handled. And the forgiveness that God proffers is no sentimental ignoring of sin. Sin matters. In face of the sin, in the very teeth of opposition, God says the impossible word, as He said at Calvary: "Be forgiven. Be no longer divided against yourself. No longer rebel against that which you were created to be." He proffers forgiveness in the very act of receiving the consequences of the sin that He forgives. " 'Father, forgive them.' "

Two men express themselves in prayer. That is indeed where we express ourselves. Before the veiled transcendence of God we show ourselves to be what we are. One justified himself. One is forgiven. (Luke 18:10-14.) Where there is no problem there can be no relevant answer. Where there is no dissatisfaction there can be no fulfillment and consequent gratitude. Where there is no sin there is no need of grace. Where there is no recognition of sin there can be no prayer for mercy. Where there is no sickness there can be no talk of healing.

But where there is recognition of sin, the frame shifts. Where there is sickness there may be healing. Where there is genuine prayer there can be forgiveness. Where the rebellion and the enmity and the violation are recognized there may be pardon. Where there is fallenness and sorrow there may be humility and request. Where there is faith there may be justification. Where there is the prayer of genuine penitence there is mercy, for God is the merciful Lord. " ' "God, be merciful to me a sinner!" ' " That prayer was heard and answered.

" ' "God, be merciful to me a sinner." ' " God has been merciful. He has always been. No love can compare with His love. His love has followed us, down the days and weeks and years, into the retreats of our own making. It has called us back: "My child, you do not belong there." His love will not let us go, even when we have thought that we most wanted to stay away from home. His love is stubborn and steadfast. He was there—with His offer of forgiveness. He was always there.

I fled Him, down the nights and down the days;
    I fled Him, down the arches of the years;
I fled Him, down the labyrinthine ways
    Of my own mind; and in the midst of tears
I hid from Him, and under running laughter.
            Up vistaed hopes I sped;
            And shot, precipitated,
Adown Titanic glooms of chasmèd fears,
    From those strong Feet that followed, followed after.
            But with unhurrying chase,
            And unperturbèd pace,

Deliberate speed, majestic instancy,
They beat—and a Voice beat
More instant than the Feet—
"All things betray thee, who betrayest Me."[5]

Three crosses stand out against a blackening sky. In the bleakness of sorrow and jealousy and death, God is speaking His word about sin. For the Son of God is upon the cross. That it should come to this! Here the world may see how God loves and how sin destroys. The cross displays before all humanity the wonder of God's love. The wonder of surpassing love! A love that is greater than hatred. And that love is for me!

If you will see what sin means—your sin—go to Calvary. And there pray, "God, be merciful to me, a sinner."

It is a prayer that God never leaves unanswered.

Questions

1. What is sin? How is it remedied?
2. What does the parable of the prodigal son teach us about God's attitude toward the sinner?

Chapter 3

Jesus Christ, the Object of Faith

God is the Christian's one object of faith. Indeed, He is the object of faith before He is the object of thought. The God who is the object of the Christian's faith appeared on earth, announcing love and calling for unconditional discipleship. Christians are defined, thus, as those who in their total life acknowledge Jesus as God.

We can come to know another person only if we disclose ourselves to him. Personal disclosure and the response to that disclosure precede personal trust. God wills to disclose Himself freely. He must be freely received. In God's coming to us He offers the great invitation. In Jesus Christ, God came into human history.

The response cannot be merely an intellectual one. It is not simply that I now know a few more facts, having heard of Jesus of Nazareth. "To think about" is not identical with "to trust in." Faith is not the acceptance of further information. It is the total commitment of unconditional discipleship.

Faith involves worship. Christians worship Jesus Christ, for they recognize that in him God has made Himself known. Jesus Christ concretely embodies the will of God as expressed in human history. He is the Word—the speaking of God.

God has acted in the life and cross of Jesus. Because God has so acted, He invites us to respond in faith. In the face of our sin we are called to responsive love for and gratitude to the God who came and disclosed Himself.

God is not known unless He is known as Lord. The God who reveals Himself is known in faith. This knowledge is not the knowledge of the pupil, but the knowledge of the disciple. So, we are not *proved* into faith. The New Testament writers *witness*. Their arguments always serve that witness. As witness is borne, God Himself draws near with the disclosure of Himself, and faith is born again.

The Christian has faith in God. There is no other object of faith. Indeed, to have faith in any other object is idolatry. To have faith in many objects is polytheism. The Christian is neither idolater nor polytheist. He has one object of faith—God.

God is, for the Christian, the object of faith before He is the object of abstract thought. For the Christian believer certain events that happened are of decisive importance for faith. The Christian way of life is not first and foremost a way of intellectual reflection. It is, rather, a way of life. The early Christians called it "The Way." They had come to have faith because of certain things that had recently happened among them. The church has never forgotten those things. It cannot forget, because what happened in the first few years of the first century is all-important for faith. God came among humanity in the person of Jesus, who was believed on as Lord. When the church has remained faithful to its Lord and when it has maintained its faith, it has always remembered that.

What happened, then, was not that another teacher came along and announced eternal truths of reason and called for adherence to a school of thinking. Jesus did not call for a mere intellectual response to a philosophy different from what had been known up to that time. In Jesus, God made demands upon human beings—demands that called for total commitment, unconditional discipleship. Jesus called for followers, not simply pupils. Response to him was not appropriated if it became only a mode of thought. Response to him was to involve a total reorientation of a way of life. Jesus' announcement was not an abstract statement about the absolute. It was the concrete call "Repent! The kingdom of God is among you!"

Something happened. Jesus came among us and announced the good news of God's love. He also made that love possible. He embodied God's love in human form. "God with us" (Matthew 1:23)—that was the event. "God was in Christ" (2 Corinthians 5:19, K.J.V.)—that is the resting place for Christian faith. "The Word became flesh" (John 1:14)—that is the unique revelation of God known to Christian faith. Jesus Christ is the unique object of faith. Jesus is Lord—that is the unique confession of Christian believers. We can never prove it. We testify to its truth. We cannot argue another into that faith. We can offer an invitation.

When we answer the question "What is a Christian?" with the response "A Christian in his total life acknowledges Jesus as God. He is one who has faith," we would have laid open the very center of things.

Certain familiar passages in the New Testament so describe Jesus. We are admonished to look unto Jesus, "the pioneer and perfecter of our faith" (Hebrews 12:2). At the close of the Scriptural canon, He is similarly described: " 'I am the Alpha and the Omega, the first and the last, the beginning and the end' " (Revelation 22:13). As the object of faith, he has invited us to have faith in him, for to have faith in him is to have faith in God. " 'Let not your hearts be troubled; believe in God, believe also in me' " (John 14:1). Jesus called for faith in himself, and faith in him was identical with faith in God, since he and the Father are one (John 10:30).

But what do we mean when we speak of Jesus as the object of faith? To enable us to understand more clearly, we shall ask for a moment that you think of some object—anything. Let us say that you thought of a ship. Now, while the idea of *ship* was in your mind, you had a specific object of thought. You can think only of that which is in some way known to you. You cannot think of what has no connection with what is within the range of your experience. To be able to have an object of thought means that you hold before your mind something that in some way you already know.

Now, let me ask you to think of a person: someone, anyone. Let us say that you thought of two persons: one whom you have never met, say, Sir Winston Churchill, and another whom you know with some degree of familiarity. You now have two objects of thought. You have read of Churchill in books and magazines and have an acquaintance with a few facts of his life, career, and character. But you do not know him as you know the friend of whom you also thought. Both were objects of thought, but with the friend there was a very important difference. The difference is that you came to know your friend differently. You have read about Churchill, but you have had personal contact and conversation with your friend. *That* makes all the difference. Your friend is not simply an object of thought but also an object of trust. You would entrust your goods and your life to that person.

The important thing to notice here is that you can come to trust other people only as they personally disclose themselves to you. If others do not will to let themselves be known, if they withhold themselves from you, they will never become objects of your trust. They may well be objects of thought, but never objects of trust. Personal disclosure comes before personal trust. The willingness to make oneself available to another precedes a genuine personal relationship.

But something else must be added to this. The one who wishes to disclose himself must be received. The person to whom the disclosure is to be made must show personal receptivity. I may be very willing to open myself in friendship to another, but unless that other individual is willing to receive and respond, no relationship of mutual trust can grow between us. The object of faith must disclose himself and must be received, that is to say, must be accepted as trustworthy.

If God is to be trusted He must make Himself known. He must disclose Himself to us. We cannot "by searching find out God"

(Job 11:7, K.J.V.). If God does not take the first step toward us, He will remain forever unknown. God does take this first step. God has made Himself known. He comes to us. In infinite love and condescension He took our mortality and dwelt among us in the tent of our flesh, being "made like his brethren" (Hebrews 2:17).

God has taken the initiative and has come to us. In that coming He offers us the great invitation. God is willing to open Himself to us. In fact, in Jesus Christ it has been done. It has become evident. Have faith in God! Trust Him. Make Him now the object of faith. He has shown Himself willing to be such. God came into human history. He calls us to trust Him and to shape our personal histories by that faith-knowledge.

It should be clear that God's demand for faith is not simply the call to add a little bit more to the fund of our information. Notice this statement: "My father has retired in the country." I am sure you understand these words. In fact, you know something that you did not know before you read them. Your fund of information has now perceptively increased. Or consider another statement: "My car is in good working order." Once again you know a little bit more than you did before. On the basis of these two bits of knowledge you can draw conclusions and implications that you could not draw before. You have something more to think about, should you so desire.

But suppose I say: "Jesus Christ is the Son of God." What then? In what way may you understand this statement? Obviously this is not just another piece of information that you can tuck away in the recesses of your mind. You can come to know what it means only as you come to know God, and *this can never be simply by learning another fact you did not know before.* There is all the difference in the world between believing information about somebody and trusting someone with all your heart. The information that you have believed may turn out to be untrue. There is such a thing as gossip and slander! But it is through trust that personhood comes into being. I may believe certain facts about Jesus, but to believe facts about Jesus is by no means the same as to trust him. Thinking about, knowing about, Jesus is not identical with trusting in him. In fact, the only guarantee that our thinking about, our knowing about, Jesus will be at all adequate is that we have already come to have faith in him. Faith must always precede correct understanding of him. Religion always precedes theology.

God comes to us in Jesus and offers Himself as the object of our trust. But we cannot create faith. We are sinners and cannot help ourselves. The God who judges us in our sinfulness offers us the gift of life. And as He does so, He calls for faith.

We have seen that this call to faith is not the call to add another piece of information to our already existing knowledge, as if we could easily acknowledge, "Ah, yes, Jesus is God's Son. How interesting! I am very grateful to you for the information," and then pass on to other things. Faith does not mean forcing oneself to accept something, adding it to his fund of information.

Faith is radical trust, the commitment of all that one has to the God who is manifest in Jesus Christ. Faith is unconditional discipleship. Faith is not "seeing the argument." It is not "believing" that a piece of information is true. Faith means accepting God in Christ as the ultimate reality by which life shall be guided, as the origin and goal of life. Faith means that Jesus becomes the Alpha and Omega of one's life, that the Christian's life becomes a life of personal trust in him.

Faith of this kind means worship. Worship is the whole-souled devotion of the trusting person to the acknowledged Source and End of his/her being. Christians worship Jesus Christ. Even the Romans knew this. A very early letter of one Roman official to another speaks of Christians assembling and singing "a hymn to Christ, as to a god." Faith means worship, and just as Jesus is the object of faith, so he is the object of worship.

We may truly worship only God. To worship anyone less is to become an idolater. The realization of this truth drove the church to strenuously oppose Arianism,* which denied the reality of Jesus' oneness with God, thus making him other than God. We know that this cannot be when we have trusted Jesus as God. If Jesus is not very God, yet I believe and worship him as such, then I become an idolater, and my devotion is misplaced.

But Jesus is also very man. For if he be not truly a human being, he has not reconciled *humanity* to God. He has not reconciled me to God. Once again my faith would be misplaced. "God was in Christ" (2 Corinthians 5:19, K.J.V.). "The Word became flesh and dwelt among us" (John 1:14). Jesus Christ, the object of faith, is true man, in whom sin is both judged and overcome. Sin is judged by God and overcome by Man. " 'Behold the man!' " (chapter 19:5). Jesus Christ, the object of faith, is very

* Arius was a presbyter in the church of Alexandria. He denied the deity of Jesus. A bitter controversy arose. Athanasius was a leading opponent. Arius was condemned at the Council on Nicaea, A.D. 325.

God, for were he not, we would be yet in our sins. On the basis of our reconciliation we confess: "God was in Christ."

We can now answer the question "Who is the object of our faith?" The object of our faith is the living God, whom Jesus Christ made known through the cross. We love him as the Saviour and obey him as the Lord.

To say that Jesus is the object of faith is to say that God has made Himself known in revealing activity. God lives for faith to be. The living, active God became a human being. God did something. He made *Himself* known. He did not send someone other than Himself to impart information about Himself that could simply be learned. He Himself came and in the revelation demanded personal trust. He did not simply shout a set of new directions to us from a lofty height and then lapse into eternal silence. Jesus is the revelation of God, God's speech. That's why we call Him the "Word of God." The Son is God speaking, and this speaking is the giving of Himself.

Something new *happened*. What was unknown became known. The mystery hidden from generations was *manifest* (Colossians 1:26). God manifested Himself. The good news is of what God did. He willed to disclose Himself so that He could be known. The *mystery* (the Greek term in the New Testament means "that which was hitherto unknown") now became known. God willed to love us. God willed to save us. God willed that we come to know His love.

Between human sin and God's salvation stands the cross. The cross did not just happen. God willed it. Between us and God stood and stands the continuing fact of sin. Between God and us stands the incarnation and the cross. Before the festal shouts and songs of joy there is the fight and the victory. That means the cross. God was in Christ. It is God who appears, who goes to the cross, who triumphs over death. And before it all and through it all is the will of God.

Jesus Christ concretizes God's will. God revealed Himself in Jesus Christ. In time we see the expression of the will of God in Jesus Christ. Jesus Christ is the external manifestation of that "mystery hidden for ages and generations but now made manifest to his saints" (Colossians 1:26). Jesus Christ is the ultimate speech of God.

What is God like? To answer this question we must look to the cross. There we see God's judgment against man, *the* Man, and through that judgment God's love for all men. We should not ask,

"What is God *like?*" For the cross does not tell us what He is like. Rather, it shows us God. God is not simply *like* Jesus. God was *in* Christ. In the activity of Jesus we see the activity of God. Through faith we see in the cross of Jesus the revelation of God. Furthermore, the God who was once made known in the Incarnation and in the cross continues to be known and loved. As the cross is preached God comes to be known and continues to be known. As witness is borne to God's reconciling activity the miracle of renewal continues to take place as the presence of the same God who was present in Jesus becomes a reality in the believer's life.

The message of Christianity is proclamation. Christianity declares that God is with us and is for us. The message of Christianity is also invitation. It says that because God has acted to redeem us, response is to be made, a decision must be made, a judgment (the Greek word is *krisis*) is necessary. God invites us to faith and gratitude—gratitude for the faith that He gives with that gratitude. Both are response to the demand of the sovereign God. Love calls for responsive love.

It is then that God is known. God is not known unless He is known as Lord. He demands nothing less than all. This is, of course, the risk of faith: that we shall lose all as we follow the demand. But, since it is God who calls us, we have no alternative choice. Either we give all or we do not. Either we let our life be dominated by a new love or we do not. Either we become a different kind of slave or we do not. There is no middle way in which we can rest with partial response or escape by failing to respond.

Thus we have come full circle to our introductory remarks. We cannot create faith. Faith is not learning some new fact about another person. The other person cannot be known unless he discloses himself, makes himself available. That is what God has done in Jesus Christ. As *personal response* is made to *personal disclosure,* the knowledge of persons takes place. *Only thus can there be personal knowledge at all.*

Such is the knowledge of the believer. And in such a manner God in Christ, by becoming the object of faith, becomes known to the believer. This is what the New Testament means by *knowledge* and by *revelation:* "that the God of our Lord Jesus Christ, the Father of glory, may give you a spirit of wisdom and of revelation in the knowledge of him" (Ephesians 1:17).

Such knowledge is not merely the knowledge of assent. It is the knowledge of faith. It is not the knowledge of the pupil, but the knowledge of the disciple. Its source is in God. Its object is His activity in Jesus (verses 19, 20). Its context is the church (verse 23).

Therefore, we can never come to faith in Jesus Christ by a process of proof. We are not "proved" into being Christians. Nor can we prove other people into being Christians. By the same token, we cannot be proved out of being Christians. We cannot prove the necessity of our faith. Being convinced that a theorem is true or that a scientific explanation is highly probable differs greatly from knowing another person. Faith is of the order of the latter. It involves personal trust.

Although we cannot prove our faith, we *can* witness to it. We can tell the story of the One who is its object and who has come to us in love. That is what the New Testament writers do. Of course they use argument and explanation, but they always employ argument in the service of this witness. The New Testament authors do not say, "We shall prove to you by the following reasons, *a, b, c, d,* that it could not have been otherwise that it was." (That approach was used by a later rationalism.) They speak quite differently. God disclosed Himself to them. What they knew was of the nature of revelation, not discovery. So they asked of others what had been demanded of them—a willing, responding heart. They witnessed. Their language is the language of testimony.

"That which was from the beginning, which we have heard, which we have seen with our eyes, which we have looked upon and touched with our hands, concerning the word of life—the life was made manifest, and we saw it, and testify to it, and proclaim to you the eternal life which was with the Father and was made manifest to us—that which we have seen and heard we proclaim also to you, so that you may have fellowship with us; and our fellowship is with the Father and with his Son Jesus Christ" (1 John 1:1-3).

Faith and Jesus Christ as its objects are commended by witness. As witness is borne, God Himself draws near with the disclosure of His personal presence. And that presence is the demand for faith, for unconditional trust.

This is the way the good news is preached. This is the way God in Christ becomes known. This is the way that I would chose to close this chapter. I would like to confess my Lord and my faith. There is nothing more certain than this: Through Jesus' death and resurrection—the act of God among humanity—my sin is forgiven and my love redirected. He has come to me, and in the great mystery of His unfathomable love He has granted to me grace so that in responding to His coming I might know Him. Thanks be to God for His unspeakable gift!

Questions

1. Explain what is meant by saying that Jesus Christ is the object of faith.
2. What is meant by the statement that faith is shaped by its object?
3. God has revealed Himself in Jesus Christ. Expound.
4. What is the difference between saying "God is like Jesus" and "God was in Christ"?
5. What is a witness?

Chapter 4

"Behind a Frowning Providence"

Life's experiences often come to us in disguise, and so we may be deceived about them. Our thinking about God may suffer as a result. Our God is holy and patient. He is a God of demand as well as of grace. He created us and makes Himself known to us as He wills, often in unexpected ways.

Faith, the distinctive mark of Christians, enables us to confess the providence of God, even in situations through which we cannot see. By faith we know of no experience outside His control.

It is easy to confess God's providence when all is going well for us. But God does not always remove the unpleasant and undesired. He wants to show us our real needs, and this He can do only as He makes Himself known.

Providence is the opposite of chance. It is God's direction of affairs, not in a general way, but in the concrete here and now of present experience. Only the eye of faith can discern God's providence. Appearances are deceptive if taken only at their face value, as at Sinai, at Calvary, and in the sufferings of the early church.

Providence may frown, but behind the frowning providence is the face of a God of love.

In face of suffering and persecution, we may have confidence in God's providence. But we must seek this in more normal days. The faith that is strong in the crisis is the faith that has been constantly nurtured during pleasant times.

God's will is done, and that will is good. Such was the conviction of Job and such is the conviction of the believer.

The measure of our trust in God is the measure of our freedom from anxiety, as well as the measure of our capacity and willingness to forgive. Joseph could forgive the great wrongs perpetrated by his brothers because he trusted in God's providence. We may trust God for what is unknown. His love directs our short and insignificant lives.

Judge not the Lord by feeble sense,
But trust Him for His grace;
Behind a frowning providence
He hides a smiling face.[6]

Did you ever change your mind about someone? You found that he was not what he seemed to be at first meeting. So you had to modify your previous evaluation. Life teaches us the important lesson that it is precarious to bank too heavily upon first impressions. All too often later experience will cause us to modify those early impressions. What seemed, with the casual introductory contact, to be so certain may indeed later prove to be quite wrong. An inauspicious introduction may be the prelude to a great friendship or a far-reaching enterprise. On the other hand, the smiling face may often be deceptive. Perhaps the disarming smile of the salesman so impressed you that you decided to buy his wares. Later you found to your dismay that the price was too high. So you returned to your smiling friend, but what a difference you noticed when you tried to explain to him the situation. The same thing holds true in religious matters. There also things may not be what they at first seem to be.

The experiences of life often come to us in disguise, and we estimate them wrongly because we are taken in by our unaided, faithless evaluation of them. Take, for example, the matter of the relation between feeling and faith. God has not necessarily come closest to us when we feel the best. Neither is He farthest away from us when we feel the worst. We cannot measure God's presence or absence, His pleasure or His displeasure, by our ecstasy or despair. Our feelings may change. God's will abides in spite of our feelings. God is greater than our heart. Our relation with the transcendent God must depend upon our setting our will toward His will, not upon the expression of happy or sad feelings.

I have deliberately chosen to write of real problems, for we get nowhere by refusing to face life in Christian terms. There is the danger of false security, on the one hand, or of false despair, on the other, if we never reckon on the real appropriation of Christian faith in the day-to-day hustle-bustle of life. Often, I fear, the Christian is no more prepared than the non-Christian to face life, often less so!

So let us ask: What do we expect our Christian faith to do for us? Give us a certainty that is otherwise unobtainable? Provide for us in our secularized mediocrity a god whom we can manipulate for our peace of mind? Will Christianity give us a vantage point from which to survey the less-fortunate multitudes? Do we expect our Christian faith to make us the master of our God? Or have we never seriously reckoned with the Christian faith in everyday life, with its share of sin and untidiness, its anger and impatience, lust and envy, its preoccupation with suffering and pain? Do we keep these real-life experiences in a separate compartment from our religion? In short, when temptation and adversity come to us, as come they will, do they find us mature in our faith?

Let us put the question in another way: What is the God like whom we serve or profess to serve? A make-believe god? Or the

God who can handle the stubbornness of an empire and at the same time draw close in condescending pity and understanding love to a harassed prophet? Is He a God who can wait when we cannot? Who is prepared to inflict, not simply to allow, pain and tribulation for the sake of His purpose for us? Does He exist for His own sake and not for ours? Does He demand a response far beyond what we dreamed we would ever be expected to make? Is He the kind of God who is apt to make us ready for such responses but then demand from us over and above anything that we have even then done? Is He a God who is easy to please but hard to satisfy? A God of law as well as of grace? Of demand as well as succour? Is He sovereign over His silence just as He is over His revelation? Does He withhold His face when He will and show it when He will? If this is the God we serve, we shall well understand why in the Old Testament He is called the "Holy God," the "eternal God," the "Most High God," the "terrible God."

Now, we must never forget that we exist for God, not He for us. Our blessedness is that in His mercy and condescension we may enjoy Him forever. God does not need us, but we desperately need Him. God is the Creator. We are His creatures. Because God created us, He will speak to us in unexpected ways. Indeed, He will speak through those media that we least expect Him to use. It is for us "frail children of dust, and feeble as frail," to devote ourselves to the divine will of unfailing love, despite ourselves and our evaluations. We must wait, ready to hear Him speak to us, and be patient if there is silence.

Frowning providence, smiling face. A contradiction? No, but it has to be experienced to be known. It is tempting to construe providence in terms of the favor and miracle that bring immediate good and blessing. But this is not necessarily so. *We cannot always understand God's way in the here and now of present experience; nor do we have to do so.* But we must have faith. The corollary of God's revelation is our faith. Just as the counterpart of speech is hearing, of visual imagery is seeing, so *faith* perceives what God is doing and saying when He is acting on us. Sometimes we understand; sometimes we do not. Faith may sometimes help us to understanding. But where it does not, faith is sufficient of itself. Faith itself is God's gift. It is the distinctive mark of the Christian. Therefore we should not be surprised when the non-Christian does not understand some things that are perfectly clear to us about God's providence. Unfaith stumbles and falters just where faith, or trust, is the most certain.

We Christians believe that God is provident or good even when all appearances appear to give the lie to the conviction. We have known Jesus as Lord and we have found the clue to life's meaning in the acknowledgment of His lordship. We have tasted and seen. And having tasted and seen, our conviction that the Lord is good, in spite of how things seem, cannot be shaken. Knowing Jesus as Lord enables us to be undeceived by the apparent untowardness of the situation. Faith in Jesus Christ means that we have a Master in those situations through which we cannot see. In fact, having such a Master means that we do not need to see through.

Christians know that the One who saves us is the one who created. The Redeeming One is also the one in whose power the world subsists. The Ultimate in the universe is the God who has come to us as our Saviour. By faith we know the God of love who is guiding the world to its proper end. The One who sees the sparrow fall is He who hung the worlds in space and who came to be our Saviour. The Basis and Upholder of all reality, the Ground of all being, comes to us in the capacity of the Saviour. Once He has met us here, all doubts as to His goodness become irrational and unnecessary. In faith we know of no experience that could lie outside the limits of His control. He who has saved us is omnipotent divinity.

Providence does not always frown, of course. Sometimes it is a smiling providence. In fact, that is the way we like to think of it. Yes, God is good when the bank account is well stocked, when the children are well, when ample provisions of food are in the pantry. Yes, God is good when the summer sunshine of prosperity smiles over the little plot of land that I call my life. Yes, God is good when health is mine and when my friends prove true and when I can see the waving corn, hear the swallows call, pick the hidden flower, and smell the sweet scents of spring. But God is good at the funeral as well as at the wedding. God is good when war and pestilence devour the reserves of a nation's labors as well as when economic prosperity sends her ships to the ends of the earth. "God is good" may be written over the portals of the hospital as well as over the threshold of the concert hall. God is good in the labor of the jailer as well as in the labor of the minister. God is good. That is the Christian's faith. God's will is the best that life can hold.

During my boyhood I read the thrilling stories in a little book called *Stories of Providential Deliverance.* The author recounted breathless snatchings from apparent death, remarkable deliverances from danger, and so forth. During such miracles it is easy to think of God as provident. But God does not always deliver. Yet His providence does not fail, although He does not deliver. Providence is not so small that it can handle only the good things of life. Moreover, it is not for us to demand the supply of our needs. God, first and foremost, exists for His own sake, not for ours. We exist, when we achieve our true end, for His glory. God has His way. It is not for us to demand, but to trust, even when we do not understand.

A very common misunderstanding of providence lurks in this territory. Of course, we look to God to provide for humanity's needs. But humanity's needs can easily become "my needs," and my needs can easily become "my desires." In truth, the correct understanding of providence enables us to see what our needs are. We do not know what our real needs are until God has made Himself known to us. We do not know what we are until Jesus Christ has become the revelation of God to us. We cannot stand apart in a neutral position somewhere and make the impartial judgment "These are my needs." We are sinful. We cannot know ourselves until God makes known what true humanity is in Jesus Christ. How, then, can we autonomously evaluate our needs?

We cannot say what our needs are; if when we try to do so we go wrong, then anything we judge about God's providence in the light of our supposed needs is bound to be wrong. Never should sinful human beings make their judgments the measure of what God should be or what God should do. That is nothing less than blasphemy. "These are my needs. If God is God, He will supply these needs. If not, He is not God. His providence is failing." We can never stand at such a vantage point and say what God should do. Never can we say what God ought to do. God always does what ought to be done. That is His nature. He is omniscient. For ourselves there are just two attitudes: faith or lack of faith, faithfulness or unfaithfulness. We trust God or we fail to trust Him.

What is providence? It is the antithesis of chance, luck, fate, fortune. If God is provident, then nothing happens by chance, even when it seems so to happen. What seems chance is not apart from the purpose of God. But since it requires faith to see the design (even in outline), one individual will interpret an event as coincidence; another person will see it as an act of God. Belief in providence means that, while the future is uncertain, even for the Christian, the conviction remains firm that what the Lord purposes will take place.

Providence is God's direction of the world, the church, the individual. He has given the power of choice to us and a certain autonomy to natural processes that makes "secular" science possible, but *His will is done.* His world and His universe never get away from Him. Such is the conviction of the Biblical writers. "He who dwells in the shelter of the Most High, who abides in the shadow of the Almighty . . . " (Psalm 91:1). " 'Can a woman forget her sucking child, that she should have no compassion on the son of her womb?' Even these may forget, yet I will not forget you. Behold, I have graven you on the palms of my hands; your walls are continually before me" (Isaiah 49:15, 16). "Are not two sparrows sold for a penny? And not one of them will fall to the ground without your Father's will. But even the hairs of your head are all numbered. Fear not, therefore; you are of more value than many sparrows" (Matthew 10:29-31).

If God directs, He directs in the here and now of present experience. If my life is now bitter or hard, I accept as God's will that I am to meet Him in the experience. This confidence in God's purpose frees me from anxiety and worry. I can trust God. But to construe God's action without faith is to misunderstand it completely. For God's providence is known only to faith. Otherwise it may appear as irrationality and meaninglessness.

At Mount Sinai, God made His gracious covenant with Israel. But smoke, thunder, lightning, and great fear and quaking accompanied it. One would hardly think that this was one of God's most precious and meaningful acts of all time if he looked only at the terrifying accompaniments. But those who had faith saw God's smiling face behind the frowning providence. Here God was entering into gracious covenant with those who were to become His people. Here He revealed Himself as their God. He promised to love them in all their experiences. He would protect, correct, and save them, making them His own possession. Here was being expressed the loving will of a holy God.

God's love was manifest upon another hill centuries later. The anger of a mad mob and the miscarriage of Roman justice called for immediate redress. Is this what happens to absolute goodness when it appears in the world? But God stood apart. The Saviour was taken from the cross and placed in the tomb, and still God seemingly did nothing. But behind the frowning providence was a face of mercy. God was eager to save to the uttermost, providing in this very act of seeming aloofness the way to salvation for all humanity.

God was present in the sufferings of the early Christians as the clouds quickly began to break over the infant church. Jewish hatred harassed the Jerusalem church. Christians were scattered, imprisoned, killed. Providence seemed to frown, but the New Testament called it the guidance of the Spirit.

Is this the sort of God we serve? The tendency is to turn away to something more manageable, to an undemanding god whom we can conveniently manage; to let the soul rest on its own mediocre level with something less than God; to create god in our image. We can manage that image, for did we not create it?

God is ready to give punishment and pain, and we become amazed that He can turn these to good. "The extreme greatness of Christianity lies in the fact that it does not seek a supernatural remedy for suffering, but a supernatural use for it" (Simone Weil). Christianity does not say, "Lord, get rid of it please!" but "Lord, use it and me for Thy good purpose." This is the response of those who have genuine faith in God. They see behind the frowning providence to the smiling face of a loving God.

And providence does frown. It frowned on *Joseph*—in an Egyptian prison as calumny spread around the court at the mention of his name. It frowned for *Jeremiah*—in a muddy well because he preached to his own fellow countrymen the God-given message that would save them from disaster. It frowned on the *Servant of the Lord*—"Yet it pleased the Lord to bruise him; he hath put him to grief" (Isaiah 53:10, K.J.V.). It was God's will for the Servant to suffer. These are some of the mysterious ways of a frowning providence, but behind it is a purpose of love, a divine plan, a smiling face.

The living God behind human woe directs events toward the best fulfillment of His purpose, even if at the time they seem irrational and purposeless, yes, even horrible and frightening. Behind them is the living God in action. "From the sight of the irrational and frightening, man should draw lessons of faith in providence, for in God the display is always a manifestation of life, and consequently a source of hope."[7]

To remember this is to know genuine strength when we are called to the vocation of suffering. Many of us will suffer in the course of our lives. Unexpectedly we could find ourselves ill and on the way to the hospital. Through no fault of their own accidents happen to the most wary. We shall all suffer in some ways. I ask you to think with me realistically and face what is, then, our Christian privilege. I do not refer to persecution for the sake of one's faith, although that might be considered, but of the Christian's attitude to pain and suffering.

When life is bitter and the sweets have departed, when drudgery and pain are mine, when loss and suffering overtake me, then I may not have the inclination, occasion, or time to build up my faith to meet the situation. I may not be ready for explanation or, indeed, be able to receive it. *The faith of happier days must strengthen me.* We must be ready now.

When we are driving and see the hill ahead that we shall have to climb, we do not wait until we are halfway up before we prepare to ascend it. We accelerate at the bottom and are then ready to change gears at the appropriate time. We prepare for the hill ahead. Wise people prepare for the contingencies ahead. So it was with the old Scottish farmer who lay on his deathbed. His daughter asked him whether she might not read to him from the Bible. He replied, "Noo, noo, lassie. The storm's up now. I theeked [thatched] my hoose in the good weather." The apostle writes: "Arm yourselves with the same thought" (1 Peter 4:1), the mind that Jesus had in face of suffering.

Almost every letter in the New Testament mentions the problem of suffering, usually in the light of persecution. Read 1 Peter with this in mind. The Christian expects reverses but has strong faith in God's purpose and providence. This is the ideal set forth. So James can write, "Count it all joy . . . when you meet various trials" (chapter 1:2).

There was a Christian attitude regarding persecution similar to that manifested toward ordinary suffering. It was an attitude of joy. Joy in suffering and death? Fanaticism and folly, so the Romans thought, and so secularists think. Their aim is security and comfort. But you and I are Christians, and our sense of values is different. (If it is not, we should seriously examine our Christian life.) Note the attitude of the apostle Paul: "Who shall separate us from the love of Christ? Shall tribulation, or distress, or persecution, or famine, or nakedness, or peril, or sword? As it is written, 'For thy sake we are being killed all the day long; we are regarded as sheep to be slaughtered.' No, in all these things we are more than conquerors through him who loved us. For I am sure that neither death, nor life, nor angels, nor principalities, nor things present, nor things to come, nor powers, nor height, nor depth, nor anything else in all creation, will be able to separate us from the love of God in Christ Jesus our Lord" (Romans 8:35-39).

Blandina, a slave girl, was tortured during the terrible

persecutions in the Gallic cities of Lyons and Vienne. She would only say, " 'I am a Christian woman and nothing wicked happens among us.' "[8] Try as they might, her tormentors could get no more from her.

Then there was Polycarp, to whom a Roman official offered freedom if he would renounce Christ. "Take the oath and I will let you go, revile Christ."

Polycarp's answer is a classic for its courage and nobility: " 'Eighty and six years have I been his servant, and he has done me no wrong, and how can I blaspheme my King who saved me?' "[9]

Whether pain or persecution, the Christian may see in the unexpected, the inexplicable, and the unjust the working of divine providence. Frowning providence—but behind it the eye of faith can perceive a smiling face. This perception does not always and necessarily come in the hour of suffering. It is given only to the eye of faith. Suffering can embitter and estrange, as well as ennoble and sweeten. Job turned bitter and angry as he thought of the meaning of his sufferings. But through the deprivation and the pain, he came to acknowledge his ignorance and arrived at a stalwart confidence in God. He found faith in the experience. It was a hard way. He finally confessed, " 'I had heard of thee by the hearing of the ear, but now my eye sees thee' " (Job 42:5).

If God is good, He is good here and now. If God directs, He directs in the here and now of present experience. And if God directs in the here and now of present experience, then nothing happens by chance, despite appearances to the contrary. *Fate, luck, fortune, chance,* are pagan words. What seems to us to be chance lies within the will of God. Faith sees through the seeming chance to God's will. Whatever takes place is inside, and not outside, the area of God's control and, so, His will. How could one bear life professing faith in God if that faith did not lead to the conviction that God is good? How can we say that we believe in God if we constantly fret and worry? The Christian religion gets rid of anxiety and care because that is not its first concern. God is the first concern of Christianity, and for one in whose existence God is the primary concern, there is no room for care and anxiety. The extent of our freedom from anxiety and from fear is a measure of the extent of our faith in God.

The measure of our trust in God is also the measure of our capacity and willingness to forgive others. I refer to one of the most touching scenes of Biblical literature, one of the few portraits of genuine greatness. Fearful and trembling, Joseph's brothers fell down before him. They surmised that he would now, after Jacob's death, turn the great power he possessed against them. Judging him by their own past, they seriously reckoned on the possibility of his vengeance. But Joseph knew the genuine power of forgiveness, because he had known the depths of genuine trust in God. He could forgive them greatly because he trusted God deeply. (See Genesis 50:15-21.) "But Joseph said to them, 'Fear not, for am I in the place of God? As for you, you meant evil against me; but God meant it for good, to bring it about that many people should be kept alive, as they are today'" (verses 19, 20).

"'God meant it for good.'" That is really all that needs to be said! Nothing more can fill out the confession. Through the byways of our life's experiences the Christian can testify, "God means it for good." We can walk on no path where God has not preceded us.

We do not know what lies in store for us as individuals. We have to trust where we cannot see. But this is not blindness. Our trust rests on what God has revealed to us in the past. "We have nothing to fear for the future, except as we shall forget the way the Lord has led us, and His teaching in our past history."[10]

We can trust God for what we do not know because we have proved Him for what we do know. We can say with Paul: "In everything God works for good with those who love him" (Romans 8:28). With Luther: "Take they then our life, goods, fame, child, and wife, When their worst is done, They have yet nothing won; The kingdom ours remaineth."[11] With William Cowper: "God moves in a mysterious way His wonders to perform; He plants His footsteps in the sea, And rides upon the storm."[12]

God's eternal love is behind your short life and mine, insignificant as they are. Will you believe?

Questions

1. Define *providence.*

2. What are some dangers to be avoided in thinking of providence?

3. Is God's will always done?

4. Could one prove the providence of God to an unbeliever? Give reasons for your answer.

Chapter 5

"In the Beginning God . . ."

"In the beginning God . . . " These words bring us to the borderland between history and eternity. They remind us that all that exists has its source in the will of God. God is not bound to the limitations of human history. Human history does not determine Him. He is transcendent. Thus His existence differs from ours, which comes to be and passes away. Out of His eternal existence God willed that human history should be.

At Creation, God did not depend upon anything to create the world. He willed to create that which, apart from His will, would never have existed. The world so created by God is good. The human body is good. Matter is not evil of itself, for it did not ultimately exist of itself. Its goodness lies in the Creator's will and act. The goodness of the creature is derived from the Creator.

"Creation out of nothing" summarizes what has just been said. All that is has its source in the unparaleled act of God's work of creation.

Christians claim to have had a unique revelation of God in Jesus Christ. Through Jesus Christ the earliest believers had come to the knowledge of God. Because of Jesus' work, they spoke of him as they spoke of God. He had performed a work of creation in their lives. The New Testament affirms that God's purpose for His creation is manifest in Jesus Christ, that the redemption of man fulfills the purpose of creation.

Because God has come to us in Jesus Christ we know of the beginning, for we were not there at the beginning. So the Fourth Gospel identifies the Word—who was manifest in the flesh—with God, who was in the beginning.

God gave the Sabbath to mankind—just as He also has given us peace and freedom and goodness. The Sabbath reminds us of God's transcendence and our own contingency, of God's newly creative act in face of human sin. Only the person of faith can affirm that God is Creator and know the Sabbath rest.

Two books in the Bible begin with the phrase "In the beginning." By means of these words, the one introduces the story of the creation of the world out of nothing. The other uses the same expression to introduce for us the eternity and divinity of the Logos, the expression of God who is Himself God—for only God can express God. In the one section of Scripture the theme is that the world was created by the Word of God; in the other that the world was led by the Word of God to the fulfillment of God's purpose in Creation. Of the One who redeemed us it has to be said, "In the beginning was the Word." Before anything else was, the Word was. But when we use the word *was* in the two different clauses, it does not mean the same thing.

We say that something "was" when, either vaguely or specifically, we can locate its position in a temporal sequence. We point out that event *a* occurred before *b* was, and event *c* followed *b*. Thus we locate an event in time. Only as we do so can we think of happenings at all. Historical thought differs from abstract thought. Historical thought is tied up with events and thus with temporal passage. It implies the possibility of locating the time when something happened and of saying that this happened before that, and that the other happened after that. And then we can make connections between the various events that we have related in this temporal way. We say, for example, that Hitler made a decision prior to the drive eastward into Russia, which took place after the Battle of Britain. Or, to use a Biblical example, we say that the drying up of the Red Sea preceded the passage of Pharaoh's army into the sea.

Having thus located events in a temporal continuum, the historian looks for relationships between the various events so connected. Here the interpretative element of the historian's work enters the picture. To make sense of the pattern of events in their temporal succession, the historian resorts to some principles of interpretation. By means of these principles of interpretation a pattern may be discerned in history.

So far, so good. An event cannot be explained unless both its antecedents and its consequences can be drawn out in a meaningful pattern of interpretation. But what if the antecedents and the consequences cannot be so discovered? Does that mean no such complete picture can be drawn? Here the historians become dissatisfied. They must know the causes and the consequences. How otherwise can they write history?

But in the words of our text, "In the beginning God . . . ," we come to the very edge of history. This scripture takes us to the borderland between history and eternity. The language of the text reminds us that history is God's creation. Before history was, God "was." Human history came into being as an expression of God's will, the will of God expressed in freedom. The expression means that there was no cause prior to God: He is the source of all that is. If we seek for an event antecedent to human history, we shall ultimately have to look beyond human history to the will of God and find there the reason for the existence of whatever is.

God is not bound to the limitations of human history. He stands above the temporal sequence in which we must do our living and our thinking. He is transcendent. To be genuinely transcendent means that at no point can God be ultimately determined—in a way in which He does not will to be—by the course of history. Because we are so determined, however, there are certain inevitabilities about our existence that we cannot escape. We cannot change the time and place of our birth. We cannot change the hereditary influences that have helped shape us to be the persons that we now are. Over such things we had no control. We are immersed in the historical process at certain points such as these.

But there is, as the old argument runs, the possibility that such contingent existence must depend upon noncontingent existence for its continued being. Once something has passed out of existence it can no longer come back into existence. (Hence the naturalist's concern about birds and animals that are threatened with extinction.) That is the nature of human existence. It must be maintained in being by God, who is not immersed in the relativity and precariousness of contingency. In fact, human existence would not have come into being except by the deliberate act of will on the part of Him who is noncontingent, that is, He who is transcendent.

Thus, human history begins when God wills it to begin. Had He not so willed, there would have been no human history. The proposal of Genesis, chapter one, is that God did so will human history. Human history (a new kind of existence, different from that of the self-sufficient and noncontingent existence of God) came to be at the instigation of the will of that Transcendent Being. Such an act is the creative act of God.

Having thus laid something of a groundwork for our further discussion, we may now say that the Biblical doctrine of Creation means first and foremost that God depended upon nothing when He created the world. The doctine is a statement about both God and man, but it is foremost a statement about God. It stresses, indeed presents, His independence of the temporal continuum that came to be at His will and word. The Biblical doctrine affirms that God is independent, transcendent. It affirms that in the freedom of His decision, He willed to create that which would never have been had He not so willed to call it into existence. The doctrine also says that human beings are contingent beings, always dependent for existence upon God. We are impotent to maintain ourselves in existence. Thus, apart from our dependence upon the Source of being, we are always threatened with the possibility of extinction, the final end of contingency.

Furthermore, the Christian doctine of Creation says that since the world is the creation of God, it is good. We must not, then, on Biblical grounds deny the goodness of the world and the goodness of the human body, with its many possible relations with that world. The world is good because it is God's creation. Matter is not evil of itself, for it never ultimately existed of itself. What did not exist of itself had its basic characteristics given to it.

So God speaks in relation to the Creation: "Behold, it is good." The goodness of the creature is a derived goodness—derived from the goodness of the Creator Himself. There can be no goodness without God, none that is not derived from Him. The creature that comes into existence from nonexistence will possess the characteristics which the Creator willed it to possess—unless some radical perversion of the creature's state takes place. For example, the creature may set itself in independence of the Creator's goodness. (Under such conditions the derived goodness of the creature may be transformed into something different. That is the meaning of the story of the Fall, but it is not our purpose to go into that at this juncture.) God is source. The creatures are dependent. They are good with a derived goodness.

Perhaps we can take the discussion one step further by looking at a theological expression that attempts to say all of this in a very brief form:* *Creatio ex nihilo* ("Creation out of nothing"). Whatever else we say or whatever else we omit to say (deliberately or not), this is the basic meaning of the doctrine of Creation: God was not indebted to preexisting matter or to any other preexisting something when He created the world. Whatever there was, and is, was owing to the fact that it was called into being by the word of God. God was not dependent upon matter that was already there and so independent of Him. There is nothing independent of God. God *is*. (Perhaps what we have here been expounding is implied in the strange name Yahweh said Moses was to use of Him: "I AM THAT I AM" [Exodus 3:14, K.J.V.].)

This being so, the act of God in creating is utterly unique. We can find no parallels—even in what we call our "creative"

---

* One is tempted at this point to explain that theological expressions attempt to set forth with as much clarity as possible the church's understanding of the implications of Christian faith. Sometimes the theological expressions become very complicated. Sometimes they are relatively simple. Most often, they themselves need explanation, because they compress much in little. That is why the creedal formulation of such expressions has been given the name *symbol*. The symbol is the meeting place of many ideas. It says much in a small compass.

moments and acts. When human beings create, we use preexisting materials. Our activities are acts of *making,* not creating. Only God can be said to create. But to shield the meaning of Creation from anthropomorphic undertones, the expression "out of nothing" is essential. Human history came into being with the creative act of God. How, then, can adequate language be drawn from our experience within such history and be applied to the transhistorical act by means of which such history came to be? "In the beginning God . . . "

But the Hebrew before the revelation of God in Jesus Christ could have said the same thing. We must now address ourselves to the crucial question Is there a *Christian* doctrine of Creation? Or to put the question in a slightly different form: Is there a particularly Christian way of stating the doctrine of Creation that we have thus far outlined?

In addressing ourselves to answer this question, we may begin by asking another: How is it that as Christians we come to make statements about God as the Creator? Or we might start another line of inquiry by asking: What does the New Testament writer mean by identifying Jesus Christ with God and by referring to Jesus Christ as the Creator? These two lines of questioning, while pursued separately, must finally meet, and in this meeting we have the distinctive Christian doctrine of Creation.

The Christian church maintains a distinctive doctrine of Creation because Christians have a distinctive doctrine of God. And we have a distinctive doctrine of God because we have a unique revelation of God. The possibility of these distinctive Christian things rests upon the expression of God's will and purpose in the person and work of Jesus Christ.

Before we speak, we must know. Before we know, God Himself must be made manifest. And when God is made manifest, we may know that it is He. He takes away our guilt and gives us a continuing assurance of His love and mercy. Before we talk about God, we know Him in experience. And when He is known there, He illuminates all of life. It is on the basis of this "knowledge" of God as one who has saved that we Christians speak of God as Creator. The distinctive Christian experience underpins all our speech about God.

This was true of the earliest Christian writers. The apostles found that in Jesus Christ, God had made Himself manifest. They found that through Jesus of Nazareth creative forces had been let loose into the world, such forces as had not been paralleled in reference to any other historical figure. Previously there had been great heroes who called for allegiance and who did great exploits, but none had offered a cure for the ill of human sinfulness. But those who responded to the call for faith in Jesus as the Christ found that through him they experienced what had come to them through no other human figure. Thus they identified him with God. Since he had introduced possibilities hitherto unknown to reside within a historical figure, they acknowledged him as none less than God Himself, and they offered him the worship due only to God. Since his work was thus creative, they identified him with the Creator. Many New Testament passages evince this understanding of him.

The New Testament writer could not speak of the Creation without taking into account the fact of human estrangement from God, sin, and the creative dealing with this radical problem in the revelation of Jesus Christ. So the New Testament affirms that the purpose of God is manifest in Jesus Christ and issues in the restoration of the distorted creation to its relation to God. The Christ-event decisively manifests the will of God and makes possible the fulfillment of the Creation, which had been twisted and broken by human perversity.

So we return to our text, this time from the Gospel of John: "In the beginning . . . " The identification is made clearly here. He who became flesh was God, and "without him was not anything made that was made." The Incarnate One is the Creator. The redemption of mankind fulfills the purpose of Creation. God created humanity to be in relation with Himself, and He redeemed us to be in relation with God, for that purpose had never been fulfilled.

Apart from the revelation of God's purpose in Jesus Christ, no distinctive Christian content could be given to the term *God* or to the term *Creation*. Without faith in Jesus Christ, how could we know of a gracious God? Without our knowledge of One who has been at the beginning, how could we know of a beginning—of *the* beginning? We were never at the beginning. We are creatures who have distorted the meaning of our existence. We live, to use the words of Dietrich Bonhoeffer, in the "anxious middle," from which we cannot step out and know the beginning. He makes the further important point: "From the beginning the world is placed in the sign of the resurrection of Christ from the dead. Indeed it is because we know of the resurrection that we know of God's creation in the beginning, of God's creation out of nothing." [13]

We who are thus caught in the fallen middle must hear God speak to us from the beginning if we are to know at all that the Creation has purpose, if, indeed, we are to know that there has been a Creation. That God has willed to maintain our existence, when it achieves its true purpose and at any cost to Himself, is manifested to us in the Incarnation and summarized in the event of the cross. The cross tells us that God, the Creator, is not the ruthless judge, but the waiting father. He is the shepherd who goes out in search of the lost and finds reason for music and rejoicing when He finds the lost.

We now turn to the meaning of the Sabbath, since the Genesis story relates the Sabbath to the beginning. God gives us the Sabbath. In this it is like everything good that we possess. Our peace and freedom and goodness are given to us by God. We have none of these of ourselves, as indeed we have no existence apart from God. Our existence is contingent and dependent, and the Sabbath constantly reminds us of our contingency, of our acceptance of dependency, and of our acceptance of God's gift of meaningfulness and life.

The rest on the first Sabbath was a part of the act of Creation. God created the world in seven days, not six. The heavens and the earth were finished in six days, but only on the seventh day did the meaningfulness of mankind's existence become clear, as it was related to the Creator. In six days God's activity had been outward and downward. One of the first acts that God asked of Adam was for him to cast his eyes upward and see whence he had come and whence he continued to exist. On the Sabbath, God, who has created humanity, now provides the opportunity for us to recognize this creative activity and to participate in this freedom, peace, and goodness by freely responding to our Creator. God asked us to do this at the very beginning of life and thus called us to a perpetual recognition so that throughout life we would find our center in the creature-Creator relationship.

Then followed the destructive activity of the creatures who were called to God's rest. And so a further creative act was required. Once again it is the case that before rest there is the creative activity of God. And once again we participate and are called to continue to participate in this creation. Again in Jesus Christ, God created out of nothing. By our sinning we had embraced nothingness and were already perishing. God acted. He entered the world of the creatures He had made, and in His decisively creative act, He gave to fallen human beings the possibility of returning to genuine being. He calls us to cast our eyes outward and upward. So whatever we have in spite of this nothingness, we receive from God. He calls us to enter into His rest. The rest on the first Sabbath, as indeed the rest on the Sabbath of each week following, thus points beyond itself. It points away from itself to the end, when God will be all in all. The meaning of the Sabbath is thus closely linked with the fulfillment of God's purposes. It is, in fact, the promise of that fulfillment.

Thus the genuine keeping of the Sabbath becomes a manifestation of hope. And genuine Christian hope knows nothing of uncertainty. It is based upon and expresses faith. Faith in Jesus Christ is the product of God's already having made Himself known to us. Thus only the individual with genuine faith understands what God's rest is and what the keeping of the Sabbath means.

Questions

1. Why is it essential for the Christian to maintain that God created the world out of nothing?

2. Is there a distinctively *Christian* doctrine of Creation? If so, state it.

3. How does the theological significance of Creation give meaning to the Sabbath?

Chapter 6

"The Just Shall Live by Faith"

Christian character can develop only on Christian instruction. The heart of Protestantism is expressed in the theme of "Justification by Faith."

To live "by faith" and "by law" are mutually exclusive ways. Faith means trusting utterly, accepting unconditionally God's evaluation of us and His remedy for our condition.

Christian faith is directed toward Jesus Christ as the revelation of God. The way of faith is a total reliance upon God. It knows no conditions.

The difficulty is that we will not admit our egocentricity. To fail to admit it leads us to a reliance upon some resource or act of *ours*. This is legalism. To think our security lies in *our* deed or thought means that we are "under law."

Faith leads us to see that we cannot rely upon ourselves in any degree. Forgiveness, acceptance, progress, are all God's gifts to be received in faith.

The initial acceptance with God by faith is justification. But what, now, after justification? Shall we strive for absolute perfection? Or shall we be content with our existing condition? The answer is to be found in the life of faith. In faith we are forgiven. In faith we conquer. We are holy—saints—as we now have faith in Jesus Christ. We are at the same time sinner and righteous.

"You are not under law but under grace" (Romans 6:14). "The just shall live by faith" (chapter 1:17, K.J.V.).

This cannot be true! Surely this is a mistake! Or perhaps Paul did not mean it as a statement of fact, but rather as the statement of an ideal—as if one were to say, "John, be a good boy," knowing that John could never possibly be what you mean by "good."

Are you really not under law? Are you really under grace? Are you really living by faith? Is this the statement of an ideal or a fact? Paul intended these expressions as *descriptions*. They describe the life of the Christian. They express the true way a Christian lives. They express the minimum requirement for Christian living. If you can't pass this test, you are not a Christian, for this is a word picture of what the Christian *is*.

But we may and *must* go on one further step. What Paul described here is the distinct Protestant Christian experience. Two revolutions are bound up in these expressions, two crises in the course of Western history that have revolutionized the world: (1)

the early struggle against a religion of works at the beginning of the church's witness and (2) the Reformation struggle against a religion of works at the close of the Middle Ages.

What amazing vitality lies hidden in a single idea! Especially when the idea has been so forgotten that its rediscovery means opening a new world of truth. Then it comes with the freshness of a new revelation, proposing the need for a decision that involves the whole person.

It is single ideas that move us, and we can only stand aloof with amazement if we do not have sympathy with the idea. If the idea does not become a part of our life, if we do not get involved in its meaning, if it does not capture and master us, we fail to appreciate its power to the other individual, the other society, or the other age. If this idea does not grip us we end up paying a homage that comes from the outside rather than experiencing a commitment that comes from inside.

Understanding is *a step toward commitment.* Failure to understand is a barrier to dedication. What is the value of a supposed dedication to something we do not understand? How can you give your whole heart to that which you do not know is really so? How may one make a serious dedication to the Protestant way of life without knowing what it is?

I suggest that understanding is a step toward commitment. Understanding something does not mean that I'm going to adopt it as my way of life or my way of thinking. I may understand, for example, the arguments of those who say that all my knowledge has come to me, in some way or other, by means of my five senses without committing myself to this view. I may understand the reason for the doctrine of universal salvation without holding it.

It is often necessary to see what is involved in a certain doctrine, way of thinking, or philosophical viewpoint in order to be in a position to reject it. If a person is not sure that some certain position is wrong, then he may very likely be holding on to some error or other that he thinks is true. And that may have tragic consequences.

It is not enough simply to *know* that something is right. Understanding is only a *step* toward commitment. When I know, I must decide. Or it may be better to say in this case that decision, commitment, and involvement are part of genuine knowledge. We would all agree with the proposition "All men are mortal." But it is not really knowledge unless it comes home to me with the impact of the personal realization "I, a human being, must die.

This life of mine, to which I cling so bravely and with such earnestness and tenacity, will one day—I don't even know when—be taken from me." There is all the difference in the world between the abstract proposition, "All men are mortal," and the concrete, personal realization, "I must die—even I." It could change one's life.

We should be clear on these important points lest anybody should think that when we start to talk about principles of faith we are being irrelevant to the life of the Christian. Instruction in Marxism makes Communists. Indoctrination in atheism makes atheists. Heretical teaching produces heretics. Christian character can develop only on Christian instruction. Protestant Christian character is based on Protestant principles. "You are not under law but under grace." "The just shall live by faith."

The trouble is that we just don't believe it. It is simply too good to be true. So we act as if it were not true and treat it as a falsehood. The result is sheer disaster.

Why disaster? Because "the just shall live by faith"! And if the just live by faith, they do not live by law. If we live by law ("under law"), we are simply not living by faith. We can try to approach God in only one of two ways: the way of law and the way of faith. *And these are mutually exclusive.* If I go to Him by law I am not going by faith. If I go by faith I am not going by law. One of these two roads leads to despair and rejection. The other leads to peace and acceptance.

"You are not under law but under grace." "The just shall live by faith." Too good, but true—a truth that has to be experienced. But first let us try to understand by asking some simple questions. What does *the just* mean? Who are the just? How does one become just, or righteous (for the two words go back to the same Greek term)? What does it mean to be righteous (or just) by faith? What is the connection between *under grace* and *by faith*? What does *under grace* mean? Why in this passage is it set in contrast to *under law*? Are these, in fact, two opposite and irreconcilable ways of trying to approach God, one (by faith) leading to Him, the other (under law) leading away from Him? Under what disguises may Christians actually be living under law when they think, in all good conscience, that they are actually living under grace by faith, and so be in danger of rejection? What is living by faith? What connection and relationship does my living as a Christian have with my being accepted by God and so becoming a Christian? What does *faith* mean?

Let us start with the question of faith. Faith means trusting utterly. Faith in God means that we put ourselves so into His care that we accept His evaluation of our humanity, His judgment upon it, and His way of handling us in our sin. Faith means that in our lost condition we let God do anything He wants with us.

Christian faith is directed toward Jesus Christ. Christian faith means that we accept Jesus Christ as the revelation of God. We trust Jesus Christ as our God. We see that we are snatched from despair and loss in Jesus Christ. We see that Jesus Christ is God giving Himself for us without reserve. Faith is an unconditional receiving of God as He forgives, judges, justifies, and condemns; as He forgives and pardons, commands and empowers. It is a total handing over of the whole personality, *relying on nothing, since there is nothing to rely on.* Such a reliance on God knows no conditions.

And here is just the difficulty. Why? What is the problem?

The problem is in us. We are stubborn rebels! Egocentric to the last, we hang on to the last vestiges of our pride until we are beaten down by the knowledge of our impotence. We want to give something to God so He will accept us *for that thing!* We assume there is some hook we can catch God by! But there is none. And your trouble and mine is that we won't admit it until the bitter end. And perhaps we never do admit that even our best is nothing. It is then that we live "under law." To live under law means that we fail to admit that the best we do is just nothing before God. Living under law is reliance—in any degree and in any form—on some resource that I have or some act that I can do.

If at any time I consider anything I do as bringing me to God *because I have done it,* then I live under law. The same religious forms that express and nurture faith can accentuate the spirit of legalism. We are not acceptable to God because we have attended the communion service, or the prayer service, or the preaching service. We are not more acceptable to God because instead of two dollars we give five dollars at the opportune time for the work of the church.

The church is not acceptable to God because it runs a high-gear promotional program, because its statistics indicate volume, or because of its expanding geographical extent. The church is not saved by its effort at all. A failure to see this leads straight into the heart of legalism, so the words "You are not under law but under grace" startle and shock us. "The just shall live by faith" should be written over every act of promotion, every decision to work for God. Without such an antibiotic reminder, the human spirit asserts itself with pride in what "*my* church" and "*my* people" have done and have. And then God rejects us.

We are saved by faith. Let us continue to be saved by faith. "Answer me one question: did you receive the Spirit by keeping the law or by believing the gospel message? Can it be that you are so stupid? You started with the spiritual; do you now look to the material to make you perfect?" (Galatians 3:2, 3, N.E.B.).* Whatever we look to, in however small a way, suggests to us that because of this deed or this institution or this program we have security—*that* is being under law. And it is a blind alley. The security it seems to bring is false.

"The just shall live by faith." Are we prepared to believe it? Or not? Faith—utter dependence—means that not a thread of self-sufficiency is left. God gives us the righteousness He demands, and we must receive it in faith. The situation is like this: I am powerless. Sin is an ever-present possibility. I am bound to sin if I rely on myself, for I am powerless. Therefore, I am to rely only on God as mediated in Jesus Christ.

But suppose I rely in faith on Jesus Christ. Will I get to the place where I will not sin? Must I expect to become sinless? Does the righteousness that comes by faith obliterate the sin that dwells within and meet the temptation that comes from without?

When believers are justified, this does not mean that it is denied that we are sinners. If a person is a murderer or a thief he does not cease to be a murderer or a thief, but because of his faith he *as a murderer or a thief* is accepted by God. Despite his past sin and present bent to sin, his faith enables God to save him.

But then? Martin Luther wrote: "Can one say that this sick man is healthy? No; but he is at the same time both sick and healthy. He is actually sick, but he is healthy by virtue of the sure prediction of the physician whom he believes. For he reckons him already healthy because he is certain that he can cure him, indeed, because he has begun to cure him, and does not reckon him his sickness as death. . . . Now can we say that he (i.e. the one justified, to whom God does not reckon sin) is perfectly righteous? No; but he is at the same time both a sinner and righteous, a sinner in fact but righteous by virtue of the reckoning and the certain promise of

---

* Texts credited to N.E.B. are from *The New English Bible*. © The Delegates of the Oxford University Press and the Syndics of the Cambridge University Press 1961, 1970. Used by permission.

God that he will redeem him from sin in order, in the end, to make him perfectly whole and sound." [14]

There will never be any point at which Christians may rely upon self in any degree. Faith is at the beginning and at the end of the Christian life. It is a life lived "from faith to faith" (Romans 1:17, K.J.V.). Failure as a Christian may be forgiven—in faith. Progress may be made toward a state of sinlessness—in faith. Acceptance with God may be had at any point in the believing sinner's life—in faith. God's gracious gift and His gracious giving are always there for us as we reach out for them—in faith.

We can be in relation with God only by faith—not by anything that we may do on whatever level before or after the encounter with Christ. There is no security in our own power or deeds. Our assurance is first and last—in faith.

"You are not under law but under grace." "The just shall live by faith." There is nothing mechanical about this. It does not mean that by giving assent to certain beliefs about God as taught by the church we are saved. It does not mean that our acceptance, on certain evidence, of truths about man or God guarantees that God's grace, like an injection, will be infused into our being. The faith of believers leads to a relationship in which we ourselves become changed. When the faith, which is God's own gift, reaches out to accept the provision of God in Jesus Christ, then our past guilt is lifted and we receive a new status with God. *This is justification.*

But now what? What is the goal of the Christian life? What lies at the end? What can we look forward to after we have been justified? Is it perfection in each aspect of life?

Our text gives the answer: "The just shall live by faith." The life of the Christian is not a life of regret for sins committed or a life of despair for perfection unattained. It is a life of assurance that in a faith relationship with God through Jesus Christ the Christian is not rejected but accepted. It is a life of trust that God forgives the past and sustains in the present. If we fall, we are forgiven—in faith. If we conquer, we rejoice in victory—in faith.

The New Testament clearly states that if believers in Christ sin, there is forgiveness and hope. "If we claim to be sinless, we are self-deceived and strangers to the truth. If we confess our sins, he is just and may be trusted to forgive our sins and cleanse us from every kind of wrong; but if we say we have committed no sin, we make him out to be a liar, and then his word has no place in us" (1 John 1:8-10, N.E.B.). "Miserable creature that I am, who is there to rescue me out of this body doomed to death? God alone, through Jesus Christ our Lord! . . . The conclusion of the matter is this: there is no condemnation for those who are united with Christ Jesus" (Romans 7:24-8:1, N.E.B.).

As believers in Jesus Christ we are to reach out unto holiness of life, even to partake of God's holiness. "Let us cleanse ourselves from every defilement of body and spirit, and make holiness perfect in the fear of God" (2 Corinthians 7:1). "To the end he may stablish your hearts unblameable in holiness before God, even our Father, at the coming of our Lord Jesus Christ with all his saints" (1 Thessalonians 3:13, K.J.V.). "But he disciplines us for our good, that we may share his holiness" (Hebrews 12:10).

What can we make of all this? The answer is found in our texts: "You are not under law but under grace." "The just shall live by faith." "The fundamental doctrine is that Christians are 'holy' because, through Christ by the Spirit, they are *in fellowship* with God and therefore, in their small and imperfect way, *like* him."[15]

We are holy—perfect—as we have faith in Jesus Christ. This is the long and short of it. We do not have to worry about our past sins; that burden has been taken care of. We do not have to worry about our future perfection; that is in God's hands. We must, however, have faith here and now. As we have such faith, God looks at us through Jesus Christ as perfect. At the same time sinner and righteous.

Too good, but true. "The just shall live by faith"—by a total commitment to God as He has become known in Jesus Christ. God unconditionally receives us. In faith before God we are righteous even as sinners. We are holy. We are perfect. By faith alone. "You are not under law but under grace." "The just shall live by faith."

Questions

1. What is justification?
2. How does the New Testament speak of sins committed after justification?
3. Comment on Luther's illustration of the sick man. What does it illustrate?

Chapter 7

By Faith Alone

Paul taught that we are justified by faith. Luther insisted that we must say we are justified "by faith *alone*."

When Paul became a Christian he wrestled with the problem of faith and the law. After preaching and raising up churches, he had to face the problem of teachers who led converts astray by insisting that they perform works of law to gain acceptance with God. These teachers were expressing the Jewish belief that God accepted those who obeyed the law. Paul saw their teaching as a betrayal of the gospel.

Paul insisted that God accepts all who have faith in Jesus Christ. He vigorously attacked the teaching that was misleading his converts. The apostle argued that Christians cannot add anything to faith in Jesus Christ when it is a question of acceptance with God. One cannot say Jesus *and* the law.

Paul worked out the implications of this belief in his letter to the Romans. Here he teaches that all are sinners. God accepts no one on the basis of law. Rather, God Himself has provided a way. God bestows what no one can attain. He accepts those to whom He gives the gift of faith. He gives His gift to us in Jesus Christ.

So the way of faith and the way of law are opposites. No one can earn what God gives. One must simply accept the gift. Paul applied this teaching to the situation of the churches in Galatia. The Galatian believers had received the Spirit when they believed. Did they want to abandon that and make the great mistake of trying to add something to Jesus Christ—to add something to faith?

What does Paul mean when he insists on faith without deeds of law? And Luther when he talks about justification "by faith *alone*"? They do *not* mean that we do nothing; that there is nothing but faith; that we can pass from faith, which is needed at the beginning of the Christian life, to other things later; that faith is the one work God accepts; that faith leads away from the church; that there are no works.

"By faith alone" excludes anything that I may depend upon for God's favor. The expression insists that God accepts only that which expresses faith. God justifies the sinner in Jesus Christ by faith and by faith alone.

Both Paul and Luther talked a great deal about faith. Martin Luther was convinced that faith stood at the very center of Paul's understanding of Christianity. Luther loved Paul's letters, for they had helped emancipate him. From studying the Pauline Epistles, Luther knew the relief that release from anxiety brought. And Paul knew what it meant to have a great burden of guilt and distress taken away.

Paul in Romans shows that all people, without exception, need

God's grace. By no means whatsoever can human beings earn what God alone can give them. And so Paul states his conclusion: "For we hold that a man is justified by faith apart from works of law" (chapter 3:28). When Luther translated this verse, he added one word that is not in the Greek and is not put in the English versions. Indeed, this same word is left out of other German translations of Romans. It is the word *alone.* Luther had rendered the passage, "For we hold, therefore, that a man is justified by faith *alone*, without works of law."

Some of Luther's contemporaries criticized him for adding the word *alone.* He responded vigorously to the criticism. He reasoned that, although the actual word was not in the Greek text, Paul's sense required it, and so he had put it into his translation.

Luther wrote: "In Romans three, I know right well that the word *solum* [alone] was not in the Greek or Latin text. . . . It is a fact that these four letters s-o-l-a [alone] are not there. . . . At the same time . . . the sense of them is there and . . . the word belongs there if the translation is to be clear and strong. . . . I was not only relying on the nature of the languages and following that when, in Romans three, I inserted the word *solum*, 'only,' but the text itself and the sense of St. Paul demanded it and forced it upon me. . . . But when works are so completely cut away, the meaning of it must be that faith alone justifies, and one who would speak plainly and clearly about this cutting away of all works must say, 'Faith alone justifies us, and not works.' The matter itself and not the nature of the language only, compels this translation." [16]

Was Luther justified in saying that "the matter" of Paul's theology demands that, when we speak of justification by faith, we say "by faith *alone*"?

We need to ask two questions. First: Did Paul speak about faith in such a way that the expression "by faith alone" truly represents his teaching? Second: If he did, what does he mean by what he says about faith? But first a word of caution and a word of welccme.

The word of caution first. Since Paul was a thinker, we have to be serious if we want to understand him. For one thing, we need to think with his vocabulary, which differs markedly from our ordinary vocabulary. Paul gave the words he used a special meaning different from our day-to-day use of them, if we use them at all.

Now, Paul had two major problems. One was his own, and the second was other people's.

First, his own problem. He was a Pharisee. He became a Christian. He had met Jesus Christ. Then he began to wrestle with his past understanding. In particular he wrestled with his previous understanding of the law. Now that Jesus Christ had revealed himself to Paul, what function did law have?

Second, there were the problems of Paul's converts. Some people say that it does not really matter whether or not you get your theology straight, provided you have faith. But that was just the problem. When Paul left his converts and entered other fields of labor, people claiming to be teachers would visit his congregations and tell them that Paul had taught them wrong. By the time these people had finished, they had left no room for real Christian faith. Often Paul's converts were left puzzled, confused, and in doubt. Some ways of thinking made it impossible to believe in a Christian way.

Paul knew that. He knew he had enemies. He also knew what they were teaching. Furthermore, he knew when he had to take what they taught seriously, when the heresy they taught was important. Sometimes he had to meet a crisis head-on, and when he did, he did so with passion. We have only to read the book of Galatians to discover that. Finally, he set out his teaching in a systematic way in his letter to the Romans.

And now the word of welcome. Come and make the effort to understand Paul. We shall have to give a little, to look at his words and their meaning, and to follow his argument from its beginning to its conclusion—to think about it and to stay close to it. For Paul had a clear and specific purpose in mind when he wrote Romans and Galatians. So if we really want to understand him we shall have to give careful attention to what he says. We must try not to introduce elements from outside. We must try not to impose a vocabulary on him. We must try to see what he means when he uses the words he chooses to use. But it will be very rewarding.

Both of Paul's problems, as we have seen, involved the problem of the law and God's acceptance of sinners. The Jewish religion was a religion of the law. Jews held firmly to three basic convictions. The first conviction was that God had revealed Himself in a particular place. That place was in the words of the Book of the Law. The second conviction was that God required obedience to the demands of the law. Disobedience was not acceptable. God revealed Himself as a God of demand. He required, "Do what I say." So far so good. But there was a third conviction: God accepted those who obeyed the law. So the job of obeying the law became the goal of life, the goal of religion. If someone kept the law, well and good. If one did not, not good at all. Jews believed, therefore, that under certain circumstances it was possible to keep the law and be accepted by God for doing so.

But what of the Christian gospel? The Christian gospel says that God is revealed in Jesus Christ. But a version of Christianity emerged that put law at the center. But, Paul argued, it was a version of Christianity that betrayed the Christian gospel.

The Jew said: "God accepts those who keep the law."

Paul, the Christian, said: "God accepts those who believe in Jesus."

Jewish Christians who followed Paul when he left on further missionary journeys spoke in his churches and said: "God accepts those who believe in Jesus *provided* they keep the law."

Paul attacked their position with all his vigor. And his answer was clear. (1) Mankind cannot keep the law. It is not a matter of this part or that part, but it is a matter of keeping the whole law—all of it. (2) Even if we could and did keep the law, God would not accept us for having done so. But since we are not able to do so, the possibility does not arise. (3) God provides a way that does not involve people in keeping the law before He accepts them. He accepts all as sinners. (4) God's saving activity (His righteousness), which the gospel makes known, is grasped by faith in Jesus Christ. (5) So we cannot say, "Jesus *and* something else." For example, "Jesus *and* the law." Jesus Christ is the *one* object of the Christian's faith. We cannot add anything to *faith* in Jesus Christ when it is a question of acceptance with God. He receives us "by faith *alone.*" (6) There are no exceptions. All are sinners. None is saved by way of law. All whom God saves are saved by grace through faith.

Paul expounded his message in the book of Romans by a careful and extended argument. He takes the reader step by step as he reasons out what it means to have Christian faith. He speaks of human sin, the divine act in Jesus Christ, and God's acceptance of humanity.

Let us summarize the first five chapters of Romans. First, Paul stated his theme. God has revealed His saving power in the gospel. This power is effective when it is received by one who has faith. Paul then explained carefully what he meant.

God is angry with the sinner, and Gentiles are sinners. But they are not alone. Jews also are sinners. So all human beings are sinners. All stand under God's judgment. Despite the law, Jews have no advantage with regard to being accepted by God. God's faithfulness is not rendered invalid because the Jews were unfaithful. The point is that no one can be accepted by God on the basis of having kept the law. So God provided as a gift that which we could not obtain by performing the works of law. God performed His saving act—showed His righteousness—in Jesus Christ. It is now possible to be accepted by God through faith.

This faith, however, is God's gift. Therefore no one who has faith can boast about it. God is in no one's debt, as He would be if anyone had worked to earn acceptance with God. God has given us Jesus Christ, who has brought justification, or righteousness. The act of that one Man makes forgiveness and life possible for all men.

Law clarifies sin and so shows up how sinful we are. But God's grace forgives the sin that the law shows up. And He does so through Jesus Christ our Lord.

Such was Paul's confession of faith. It was a theological statement. It was in direct opposition to the teaching of those men who came into Paul's churches and misled his converts.

Several things stand out clearly from this brief summary of Romans. (1) God has acted in Jesus Christ. God has shown Himself in Jesus Christ. God has revealed His righteousness in Jesus Christ. That means that God has performed His great saving act in Jesus. Jesus Christ is central. (2) All human beings are sinners. (3) There is no way from humanity to God, no way at all. The way of law is a blind alley. It does not lead to acceptance with God. Any way that leads to God comes from God. (4) God has provided the way of faith and has made faith possible. God accepts the person who believes. (5) Those who exercise faith and who experience acceptance with God confess that it is God's doing. It is all a gift of God's grace.

Paul spoke from experience. He knew the frustration and futility of relying upon the way of law. He had also experienced acceptance with God through faith. He called that experience of acceptance *justification*. So the way of law and the way of faith are opposites. Either acceptance with God is an accomplishment or it is a gift. You either achieve it through obedience to the law or you receive and accept it as a gift of grace. It is a matter of either/or. Either earn your acceptance by keeping law or receive your acceptance as a gift of God's grace. The act of receiving, Paul called *faith*. It is unaccompanied by works of law. So Paul stated his conclusion: "For we hold that a man is justified by faith apart from works of law."

This was the passage that Luther translated by adding the German word *allein:* "For we hold, therefore, that a man is justified by faith *alone,* apart from works of law." Luther was right. He wished to make emphatic the opposition that Paul was teaching. He wanted to stress the total distinction between faith and anything other than faith, in particular between faith and law, faith and the doing of deeds that some believed put God in one's debt.

God through Jesus Christ offers His gracious gift. It is not a matter of doing anything to earn what God gives. Here nothing counts, for nothing can. Any attempt to match what God has done would be impertinent and impossible. A gift remains such only if we accept it. It ceases to be a gift if we try to pay for it. To say, "Thanks very much, but I'll pay for it," changes the whole relationship. So Paul's "apart from works" and Luther's "by faith *alone*" insist that the relationship with God in which we are accepted is a gift received by faith. Anything other than faith is quite irrelevant.

Before concluding this chapter, we should make two important denials about faith.

First, faith is not simply assent. In the English language we use the term *I believe* in many different ways. Most of these have nothing to do with the faith of which we are speaking. We say, for example, "I believe that it was John who spoke to me." What we mean is that, while we are not sure, we think that this was probably the case. We say, "I believe what you say." What we mean here is that I accept what you say as true. We can believe a person's words and never have met the individual. We say, "I believe in penicillin." We mean that, given certain circumstances, we have confidence in its healing properties.

But none of these approaches the Christian meaning of "I believe." We get nearer to its nuance with such a usage as "I believe in you, Dad!" Here a son or daughter expresses personal trust in his or her father.

When "believers" speak of faith in God, they are talking of trust, for which the child's confidence in his or her dad is an analogy. Christian faith is the unconditional trust of those who put their confidence, for life or death, for redemption, for present and future, in the care of the God whom Jesus Christ made known.

Faith is not just mental assent to a fact. Christian faith is not thinking that it is probable that certain things are true. Faith is not, for example, accepting as probably true that a man called Jesus lived and died at a certain time in history. Nor is faith a sort of wager that one takes in an emergency when there may be little alternative. Faith is not like trying a new drug when nothing else has worked, hoping against hope that this time you have found healing. Faith is personal trust.

Second, faith is not a work. It is not the one work that saves us. Indeed, it is not a work at all. Faith is not *the* work God accepts in place of other works that we find it impossible to do or that we do and think God accepts. Faith is God's gift. It is the creation of His free grace. Yet we must have faith.

We have now moved to a positive statement as to what faith is. It is God's gift. Faith is also my act, not an arbitrary act that makes life irrational, not an act unrelated to the rest of human activity and thought. Faith is an *integrative* act. It creates a central point of reference for all of life's other acts. It centers one's personality in God. It centers one's thought and activity around the service of God and of one's fellows. Faith, by providing the resources for consistent action, makes life whole. Some of the acts we did, we no longer do. To do them would disrupt the harmony that faith brings into life. Now all our acts have a central point of reference. Life has been simplified. The life of the Christian is one of progressively becoming whole, unified as faith works itself out in every aspect of our living.

When Paul heard what was happening among his churches in Galatia, he realized that the situation was so serious that he must quickly do something about it. His converts were being turned away from the faith. He could not understand how they could so quickly turn from his teaching to a different, alien teaching that led them away from faith, away from Jesus. So he acted with passion and speed. He later developed these same ideas in the book of Romans.

Once again notice the main outline of his reply. (1) No one is accepted by God by performing works of law (Galatians 3:10; 2:16; 5:2). (2) Justification is not by way of law. If it were, Jesus "Christ died to no purpose" (chapter 2:21). (3) When Paul first came to Galatia he spoke about faith. The people responded and experienced acceptance with God and the endowment of the Spirit, which was God's gracious gift (chapter 3:1-5). How could they go back on that? (4) Once you start on the way of law you have to go the whole way. If you accept the need for one work of the law, then you have abandoned Christ for the way of law (chapter 3:10; 5:2). (5) So there is a choice. That choice is between "Jesus only" and "Jesus and something else." That something else might involve living like a Jew, for example. That was Peter's mistake, and he was to blame (chapter 2:11-18). A believer does not have to live like a Jew in order to ensure acceptance with God. That is like trying to put together gift and debt, faith and law, grace and payment. To say, "Jesus and something else" (whatever the something else is) is to repudiate the gospel.

No wonder, then, that Paul reminded his Galatian readers of their first encounter with Jesus Christ and their first experience of the Spirit. "Let me ask you only this: Did you receive the Spirit by works of the law, or by hearing with faith?" (chapter 3:2). Which was it? Jesus *and* something else? Or Jesus alone? By faith *and* something else, or by faith alone? Chapters three and four of Galatians represent Paul's attempt to work out in various ways that it was by faith and not at all by deeds of law that the Galatians had found acceptance with God.

The phrase "by faith alone" is open to misunderstanding because it is short and condensed. Because it is so succinct, we need to say some of the things that it does not mean.

1. "By faith alone" does not mean that we are to do nothing. God's grace does not excuse us to become indolent and slothful. We misunderstand faith if we think that it relieves us of all effort and striving. Faith does not tend to cheap grace, "the deadly enemy of the church."

2. Nor does "by faith alone" mean that there is nothing but faith. Christianity is a way to act, a way to worship, and a way to think. Many things are connected with the Christian revelation.

3. It does not mean that faith is alone at the beginning of the experience and that then we pass on to other things. We must not simply fix faith to justification at the inital point of the Christian life, the initial acceptance with God. The relation once established is maintained by faith.

4. "By faith alone" does not mean that faith is the one work that is acceptable to God. For faith can be made into a work. "By faith alone" does not mean "by one work alone, that work being faith."

5. We must not think that the believer may rely on faith and become dissociated from the life of the church and from those means that are the vehicles for nurturing and communicating faith within the church: the Scriptures, the preaching of the Word; the

sacraments; the church's work in the world. Faith is not alone in the sense that it makes the believer a loner.

6. It does not mean that there are no works. "By faith alone" does not exclude; it includes. There are two kinds of work: works of faith alone and works of law—works alone. Works are exclusive. Faith is inclusive. Faith includes within itself, so to speak, all the works it enables the believer to do.

We may get some help in our understanding of faith if we think of another important Reformation principle: "The Bible and the Bible only." This is a fair English translation of the Latin phrase *Scriptura sola.* Notice that the word *sola* occurs here as it did in the faith phrase, *sola fidei.* The two are parallel, and in understanding one we may find ourselves better understanding the other. In some respects the one says everything but faith is excluded. In some respects the other says everything but the Bible is excluded. In what respects?

"The particle 'alone' can only be properly understood when one knows what is meant to be excluded, and in what respect. It would be nonsensical to regard the Reformation slogan 'through faith alone' as excluding works altogether. *Works are only excluded from that on which before God I may depend.* Similarly it would be nonsensical to regard the Reformation slogan of 'Scripture alone' as allowing, say, the minister to give up reading theology with a good conscience, or as forbidding the pious Christian to read any other literature, on pain of a bad conscience. Rather, the principle of Scripture is intended simply to exclude, absolutely, any other witness in the matter of faith as binding save that which appeals to Scripture and submits to its authority."[17] (Italics supplied.)

Scripture stands alone. It is unique as the primary witness to Jesus Christ. All Christian experience and faith depend ultimately upon that witness. There is no other such book. Similarly, faith stands alone. It is unique in that it excludes any and all works to which I might appeal to gain God's favor.

The Reformation principles do not mean that there are no other books or no works. They do mean that, on the one hand, there is no other such authoritative witness and reference point for the Christian, and on the other hand, that whatever works the Christian believer does, they are acceptable to God only if they are an expression of faith.

So faith stands alone and unique. The Christian's life is the life of faith. That means that the Christian's faith in Jesus Christ takes over one area of life after another until the whole is colonized. Faith is brought into and expressed through every feeling and activity and thought until it touches the whole life. All that is acceptable to God is an expression of faith. The Christian lives by faith alone. There is a priority about faith. Nothing else can displace it for whatever reason and at any time in the life of Christians if they are to remain genuine Christians.

"By faith alone" means God alone. It is not "faith alone," but "*by* faith alone." Faith is the vehicle for God's presence in the life of human beings. For the Christian, "by faith alone" means that God is present through Jesus Christ in forgiveness. Faith in Jesus Christ is faith in God. Faith has God as its object, and forgiveness as its result. Only God can forgive. There is no vehicle of forgiveness but God-given faith. The gift of guilt's removal is channeled through faith. Works terminate in themselves; faith terminates in God. Works have their source in self; faith has its source in God.

And the miracle remains. The lifting of the burden of guilt is a present reality. Faith is living. God lives for faith to be. That is what the doctrine of the Trinity says. God lives. Jesus is risen. The Spirit is present in the church and in the world. You may be forgiven.

Have faith in God. Put your trust in Him. Take the risk of committing yourself to the promise of His grace. You too may know His favor. You too shall live in His favor. You shall know that, in faith, all sins are forgiven; all life is centered, meaningful; all men are brothers; and God is good. You shall know and continue to know *by faith alone.*

You too shall know the quietness in the storm; the Presence in the valley of the shadow; the persistence of courage through the threatening; the abiding of meaning in the chaos of irrationality. You too shall know all because you know Jesus Christ *by faith alone.*

You too shall know the recurrent miracle of a persisting faith. Once and again you stand in awe before the Almighty and bow in gratitude before the cross. *There* life's question is answered, even if many of its questions remain unanswered.

Questions

1. What does the phrase "by faith alone" mean?
2. What is a legalist? Why is legalism a denial of the Christian gospel?
3. Attempt to define and illustrate what *faith* is. Distinguish *faith* from *belief* and *assent.*

Chapter 8

The Works of Faith

The question " 'What must I do to be saved?' " can be interpreted in such a way that it becomes a demand for some kind of work to effect salvation. The apostolic answer, " 'Believe in the Lord Jesus,' " shows that this is the wrong way to ask the question. Faith is a deed that has to be done, but it is not the same kind of deed as one that is done to gain salvation. I cannot "have faith" as I can say a series of prayers or go on a pilgrimage. "Have faith!" That which is the opposite of all self-sufficient deeds must be done. This deed of faith is God's work in us. God accepts only that work which His grace has enabled us to perform.

Faith is not the one work that God accepts in preference to other works. It is not such a work at all. It is God's gift to us, and since in our incapacity God grants grace to fulfill His will, there is no room for claim upon Him on the basis of our deed. Faith is not a work of that sort.

All Christian works are the works of faith. Having faith, we do works of all sorts. God accepts us for the faith that is His gift. There is no other basis of acceptance with Him. We cannot, then, set faith over against works.

In a sense, we are denying "works" to make room for works. Christian works result from faith. A legal work is a deed done out of our own resources, by means of which we seek to put God in our debt. By God's grace we are enabled to do a work of faith rather than a work of unfaith, in the hour of temptation, say, to impurity or to impatience. We are not accepted for what we do. We can do only when God has accepted us. God rejects what is not of faith.

Thus we avoid two errors: that which says there are no works (and may lead to spiritual laziness) and that which says we are accepted for what we do. Since grace is always necessary, we never outgrow the appropriateness of gratitude.

When the heartfelt cry of the harassed jailer reached the ears of the great apostle it met with a unique response. To his question " 'What must I do to be saved?' " Paul answered, " 'Believe in the Lord Jesus, and you will be saved' " (Acts 16:30, 31). It was not the first time someone asked that age-old question. Nor was it the last. "What must *I* do?" What activity will bring the coveted state of mind? Tell me the kind of actions that will put the restless heart at peace. Give me the prescription for panacea! What must I *do?* The cry constantly recurs. Surely there must be some kind of activity that will bring satisfaction in the brokenness of existence.

The question has been asked in many different forms and at different times. And many answers have been given. Many different activities have been prescribed. Go on a pilgrimage; give away your money; go without food; inflict pain upon yourself; say certain prayers at certain times; believe in certain ways; accept the authority of certain teachings; and so we could go on.

But what does the question mean? If it requests the prescription for a certain kind of activity within the compass of human capacity, then it is a cry for a means of self-salvation. It thus means, "Show me something or other that is within my power to accomplish and for which salvation either will be given as a reward or from which it will follow as an inevitable result. What must *I* do?"

If the question means that, then the answer must show that the question is wrongly conceived and must be corrected. "What must I do?" "You must have faith." But the faith that is demanded is not a plant that grows on mortal soil. It is not a manifestation of some human capacity or other. So the answer, "Have faith," needs reevaluation. How may I believe? That was not the kind of work for which I was looking. I was expecting to be directed to something that I could do. But to have faith—what sort of deed is that?

What sort of deed is faith? This is a worthwhile question. Obviously, it is not the same order of deed such as those mentioned above. It is not in the same class. Because it is so different, we hesitate to call it a deed at all. For we cannot *do* it. If you say to me, "Say so many prayers for a week" or "Consent to what I shall now impart to you," I can ready myself to respond and drive my will to response. If I am told to give so much money to a certain cause, I can likewise, with some effort, command my volition to the task. But to have *faith!* That is no work which I can so perform. Indeed, it is not a work at all. I cannot brace myself to exercise faith. I cannot force myself, against my will, to a deed like this.

But our text reports that "Believe" was said in response to a question about a deed to be done for the benefit of salvation. "What must I do?" "Believe! That is what you must do." That which is the opposite of all self-sufficient deeds must be done. The activity that puts a minus sign in front of all striving activity must be performed. Without it the question has no answer.

Here we meet with the paradox of doing. We must have faith, for without it no salvation is possible. But on the basis of the believing, nothing can be claimed from God that is not already the gift of His grace. Not even the faith by means of which that grace comes to us. The "work" of faith that we must "do" is God's work in us. "For God is at work in you, both to will and to work for his good pleasure" (Philippians 2:13). Only within the context of God's prior activity can any work that we might do be acceptable with Him. God accepts only that work which His grace has enabled us to perform. God receives only that labor which is done through faith, and that faith is, in the first place, His gift to us.

So God works in us what we work out (verses 12, 13). Only so is any work of any value. Its value is derived, not innate. A work is accepted, not because it is done, but because it is done in faith as a response to God's grace. I cannot count my works done and rejoice in my acceptance, which really means self-sufficient pride in my prowess. Rather than count, I give thanks for the depth of God's mercy that enabled me in spite of myself. Grace and faith are qualities, not quantities. They are a relation, not a substance.

Faith there must be. "Without faith it is impossible to please" God (Hebrews 11:6). But faith is the negation of all claim. It is not the one work which we are able to do that God accepts in preference to all other such works. Faith is not a work of such a kind at all. If we speak of it as a "work" at all we must give the word *work* a most unusual meaning. We must believe, but the faith by which we believe is God's gift—it is not a human work. God does not count it in preference to other works.

Faith is a work we must do, but we cannot do it except God grants us grace. "For by grace you have been saved through faith; and this is not your own doing, it is the gift of God" (Ephesians 2:8). We are to believe, but faith is God's gift. We are to repent, but "the goodness of God leadeth . . . to repentance" (Romans 2:4, K.J.V.). We are to obey, but we cannot obey apart from the enabling power of God, given to us in our very desires after obedience. We are "wretched" men, "captive" men, imprisoned within the "body of death," slaves to "righteousness" (Romans 7:23, 24; 6:13). Yet in our state of inability come the imperatives: Repent; be converted; obey; believe! Since in our incapacity God grants grace to fulfill His will, there is no room for claim upon Him on the basis of our deed. Faith is not a work of that sort. We must do it. But we can claim no good for having done it.

We must now go a stage further. All the works that Christians do are works of faith. No others have any importance to Christians. There is no work that can be done independently of God's grace. There is no work for which we can claim credit. All our works are works of faith. He accepts us for the faith that makes such works possible, not for the works we actually do. God recognizes only two classes of persons: *not* those who do more works and those who do fewer; *but*, rather, those who believe and those who do not.

" 'What must I do to be saved?' " " 'Believe in the Lord Jesus, and you will be saved.' " That is the long and short of it. Faith: first, last, and everywhere. God accepts us, *not* because we do the deed, but because we are the kind of people who have faith and who in faith perform the deed. He accepts us for what we are—believers. As believers, we do works, the works of faith. God accepts our works because they are done by those who believe. They are otherwise unacceptable. In fact, to the eye of unfaith the works of the unbelieving may seem more impressive than those done by the believing, for we are apt to judge in terms of quantity, ostentatiousness, and public opinion.

The parables of the Pharisee and the publican and of the sheep and the goats correct the faithless evaluation of showy deeds. The Pharisee listed what he did—his weekly routine of religious works. The publican, in abject humility, confessed his faith in God. He was justified; that is, God accepted him. The Pharisee and his works were repudiated. Why? They were not the works of faith. So with those rejected at the scene of the last judgment. "Did we not do this and that and, moreover, the other?" "I never knew you!"

The summing of deeds—however public, private, or even subconscious the process—done without faith exhibits pride and earns rejection. The humble confession of unworthiness in faith receives as a gift God's gracious acceptance. It is not what we do but what we believe that matters. If we add up anything, let it be our sins. Then we shall be driven to faith. God accepts us for the faith He gives to us. There is *no other basis* of acceptance with Him.

It is obvious that when we realize this, we can never set works over against faith as if they were polar opposites. It is not a matter of *either* works *or* faith. Rather, it is *both* faith *and* works. Faith never stands alone. Works always accompany it. Faith and obedience are inseparable. But "works" may stand alone. Faith never can. Because this truth is so often misunderstood, people sometimes become concerned when they hear a sermon on righteousness by faith. They ask the preacher when he will talk about works. They insist that righteousness cannot be by faith alone. So deeply has a reliance upon what we can do taken first place that to insist on the genuine priority of faith tends to frustrate and puzzle us. Of course there are works! When we say "justification [or sanctification, for that matter] by faith alone," we do not exclude obedience. Instead, we exclude a certain kind of works. We are denying "works" to make room for works!

Nothing but confusion, frustration, and puzzlement can issue from confounding the two kinds of works. We must distinguish clearly between them—so that we may deny the one sort and affirm the other. The works that we deny are those which lead us to feel satisfied with ourselves. They are those that we can think of without faith. They lead us to rely upon human resources, and we think of a reward being given. The same act—let us say the giving of an offering—can be done in either of two ways. An act does not become an act of faith simply by being performed within a religious context. Nor does an act of faith cease to be such when performed in the secular world. Any work that the Christian does either expresses faith or it does not. If it is not performed in faith, it is a barrier to faith and not a vehicle for its manifestation. It may appear identical with an act of faith, but appearance is not trustworthy.

Consider, for example, the Christian virtue of patience. Patience does not imply taking whatever comes in a resigned attitude of passivity. Patience is virile and energetic. It is that persistence in fortitude which deals constructively and creatively with pain, criticism, suffering, and misfortune. Patience is the fruit of a faith that endures and that has its source in God's grace. God does not reward us for those acts that we do in the patience of faith. They themselves are reward enough, but reward and merit are not appropriate in this matter. For such works are not the product of our own resources, but of God's grace.

And so with any of the works performed by the believer. The believer is enabled to do them; God gives what He commands. In our works of faith we bear back before God that which He has given to us. "We give Thee but Thine own, Whate'er the gift may be." The works that Christians do are what God has enabled them to do. God commands us to do them, but they cannot be done by an external response to command. In the words of an ancient prayer, "Give what Thou commandest and command what Thou wilt."

The work done in response to God's command is the work of faith. No other work is acceptable, for no other work is given. All other deeds are works of law, works of self. These are always rejected. Of the doers of such works He says, "I know you not." And His response occasions great surprise, but our concern is expressed by a final appeal back to the works that we have done. " ' "Did we not prophesy in your name, and cast out demons in your name?" ' " (Matthew 7:22). Look at what we did, and accept us for that. Jesus answers with an emphatic negative: " ' "I never knew you" ' " (verse 23).

Interestingly, this passage speaks of unacceptable works. Jesus prefaces the passage by stating that the one who enters the kingdom of heaven is " 'he who does the will of my Father who is in heaven' " (verse 21). The works they had performed did not correspond to the doing of God's will. There are "works" and works. It is not a matter of mere activity. The activity must reflect God's will and a response to it. That is the vital matter. "Whatever does not proceed from faith is sin" (Romans 14:23). It is a hard saying, a stumbling block!

By speaking thus about works of faith we avoid two extremes, both of which have had and still have currency in Christian circles. On the one hand, we avoid the error that denies the need for any works in the name of faith. "Solafidian sloth," * some have called it. By laying the stress upon faith we insist that whatever works are done and will be done (spontaneously, not because they must) will root from faith. So we may speak of both "by faith alone" and "the works of faith."

On the other hand, we avoid the ever-present error of seeking for acceptance on the basis of what we do. This latter attitude assumes that we have the capacity to do that which God will be happy to accept. It implies that grace is not necessary, that we have native resources to do the will of God. We are thus led to think that what we do makes God a debtor. This is legalism, Pelagianism, works-righteousness. We deny it in the name of faith. God is never in our debt. We always rely upon His grace. The faith by which our works become possible comes as a gift from God. We never get beyond the need for submission and humility. We never outgrow the appropriateness of gratitude.

Questions

1. Distinguish between works of faith and legalistic works.
2. Explain the passage "The law does not rest on faith" (Galatians 3:12).

---

* The idea that God accepts a person on the basis of faith alone led to the false conclusion that the person so accepted had nothing to do. Both Paul and Luther had to face this problem. They both protested about the conclusion drawn, namely, that the believer could be inactive or slothful. The adjective *solafidian* refers to the formula *sola fidei,* which means "by faith alone."

3. Carefully differentiate between two senses of the term *law*. What is the importance of this distinction?

4. Why does gratitude characterize Christian faith?

Chapter 9

The Nature of Christian Obedience

We must speak of law and obedience in such a way as to make clear that all that the law requires is superabundantly fulfilled in Jesus Christ.

Two conclusions go wrong, but in opposite directions: (1) that when Christians speak of law, they are engaging in a display of legalism, and (2) that if Christians do not always speak of law, they are antinomian and libertine. On the one hand, by running away from legalism we may end up with cheap grace. On the other hand, by fleeing from cheap grace we may end up with legalism.

The important question is *How* do we come to acknowledge the authority of law? Two answers may be given to this question: (1) to hear and to understand the propositions is enough, or (2) it is only in faith that we can know the authority of law. If law is a means of mediating God's will to us, it is because God comes to us through His law. So we must talk about law within the context of God's revealing Himself to us.

The term *law* can have one of two meanings: (1) an injunction or an imperative that sets out for us certain demands, or (2) an attitude of legalism. The believer affirms the first meaning of law, but repudiates the second meaning. The law is to be kept, but not legalistically. Christians keep law, although they are not "under law." The apostle Paul denies that we are under law. He also states that Christianity does not make void the law. The law is not of faith, yet obedience is insisted on. We can conclude, then, that faith is opposed to law in the one sense (legalism), but that it leads to the confirmation of law in the other sense (imperative). *What is called for is the obedience of faith.*

Christians are concerned about God's will for them now. Their fulfillment of it is both personal and present and is performed in gratitude. Christian obedience does not end in a series of commandments. It has its source in the living God, whose commandments are "exceedingly broad." God gives what He requires. The obedience that receives is total. Thus law is fulfilled, while law is excluded. Moreover, provision is made for forgiveness, and there is none of that "under law."

Whenever one speaks of God's grace and the life of faith and presses the Biblical truth home that human beings are utterly dependent upon God and receive everything as God's gracious gift, someone will express the anxiety that the emphasis is disturbing. After all, do not we have to *do* all kinds of things? We have to obey, do we not? There is law just as surely as there is grace, is there not? To a people used to hearing about the importance of law (did not Ellen White say that Adventists have spoken about law so much that their souls are filled with dryness?

See *Review and Herald,* March 11, 1890.), the gospel of grace sounds strange. We must try to understand why this is so. And we must come to see that all that the law requires is superabundantly fulfilled in Jesus Christ. We need to recognize that the context within which we speak of law determines how we shall speak of it. It determines whether when we speak of law we shall be legalistic or not.

Two conclusions are often drawn concerning the law. Both are quite wrong, but wrong in opposite directions. The first is that whenever Christians speak of law, they are engaging in a display of legalism. The second is that if Christians do not always speak of law, they have no basis for obedience. Most likely they are antinomian and libertine! Although each position is extreme and exaggerated, there is reason why each has been made possible. The law has too often been presented as if it were first and foremost, and as if concern with adherence to law was the primary matter. When that happens, grace and forgiveness recede into the background, with disastrous results. The letter of the law becomes more important than the spirit, and the centrality of Jesus Christ becomes forgotten.

In the second case a reaction against such legalism has at times led to a deemphasis upon obedience. Grace has been cheapened. The cost has been so lowered that discipleship has become no harder than membership in a club. We often forget that while God freely gives us His grace, it costs no less than all. The gift of God is the great demand for everything. The church is always in danger of cheapening grace. We must constantly be reminded that sacrifice and self-giving lie at the center of discipleship. We must take up the cross. We must follow Jesus. But it is of vital importance *how* we shall avoid this danger of cheapening God's grace, for if we are not careful we shall fall back into the other extreme. In avoiding cheap grace we may run right into legalism.

So we must avoid two threats at all costs. The first is that in running away from legalism we turn into libertine and antinomian proponents of cheap grace. The second extreme is the opposite of this: In fleeing from cheap grace and antinomianism we may end up in legalism. We must clearly and emphatically discover *how* we may speak of discipleship and obedience so that we shall avoid both a legalism that excludes grace and an antinomianism that cheapens it. We must not end up repudiating God's grace, denying faith, and setting up self in place of God's will.

For many years Seventh-day Adventists have insisted upon

keeping the Sabbath. Other Christians have often understood this demand as being legalistic. Now, one can present Sabbathkeeping in a legalistic manner. The argument runs: The law is to be obeyed; the law speaks of the seventh day as the Sabbath; therefore, the seventh day is to be kept as Sabbath. *Ergo,* what are you going to do? Obey or disobey the law? Obey or disobey God?

We must recognize that *the context of such an argument is all-important.* It is to that context which we must give careful consideration. We can carefully consider the context by asking: How do we come to acknowledge the authority and binding force of the law? We can respond in one of two directions. On the one hand, it may be said that the recognition of the authority of the law is *intrinsic.* To hear and understand the propositions is enough. The next thing is to get on and obey it. By contact with the law alone we come to recognize its claim upon us and are thus led to obedience. On the other hand, it has been said that the recognition of the authority of the law is *extrinsic.* We cannot appreciate and fulfill the demands of the law, putting ourselves under its authority, apart from faith in God.

Now, if the authority of the law were independent of God, there might be some plausibility in the claim to follow it apart from Him. But we must not give the impression that the law is *to any extent* independent. Whatever instrumentality may be the occasion for our encounter with God, we always encounter Him directly. If law is a means for mediating God's will to us, it will be because God comes to us through it. God is always known directly, through whatever means He comes to us. So we must set our thinking and speaking about law and its authority firmly within the context of God's revelation of Himself to us. By so doing we can avoid the two extremes that say either the law is all-important or it is of no importance.

But we need to clear up what we mean by *law.* The word can be used in two senses: (1) of a law that sets out certain requirements or (2) of an attitude of legalism—following law for the sake of security, safety, or reward. Obedient Christians do not have to lapse into legalism. We may keep law, yet not be under law. Legalists accuse the Christian of being antilaw, antinomian, because they fail to see this. They think that when the person of faith says that Christians are free from law, he is talking about law in the first sense and is thus repudiating any kind of demand. But that is quite wrong.

The believer says two things: "We are not under law," and

"The law is necessary." In fact, the apostle Paul expressed this aparent paradox. "You are not under law but under grace" (Romans 6:14). "Do we then overthrow the law by this faith? By no means! On the contrary, we uphold the law" (chapter 3:31). (In neither case does the apostle use the Greek article. He speaks of "law," not "the law.") The ambiguity becomes stark and patent. You are not under law. Law is established.

How can this be? It is certain that the way to God is the way of faith. Moreover, God gives us that faith, and it is the antithesis of law. "No man is justified before God by the law; for 'He who through faith is righteous shall live'; *but the law does not rest on faith*" (Galatians 3:11, 12). The antithesis could not be more sharply drawn. Law and faith are polar opposites. Yet the New Testament throughout insists that obedience always accompanies faith. We are thus driven to conclude that faith is opposed to law (in one sense), but that it leads to the confirmation and establishment of law (in another sense). The obedience called for is the obedience of faith.

The God of faith is holy and just. He will not compromise the demand He makes upon the believer when He calls for faith. It is the legalist who relativizes the demand. Adherence to certain requirements in order to be accepted is quite different from fulfilling the total demand because of heartfelt gratitude. *The legalist never knows genuine gratitude. The individual of faith knows nothing else.*

Christian obedience is the obedience of faith, the gift of God's grace. It is the response of the total being to God's all-encompassing demand in Jesus Christ. Wherever God expresses His will the Christian responds spontaneously. The obedience of the Christian does not terminate in a series of injunctions. It has its source in the living God. Thus faith does not inquire, "What *was* the expression of God's will?" but rather, "How may I *now* know God's will?" There is nothing static or perfunctory with genuine Christian obedience.

Such obedience is unreserved. It involves total committal to the absolute will of God, however it is revealed. Because God's will is absolute, we must always resist the temptation to relativize it, to accommodate that will to our desires. We must refuse to say that what we do is the will of God when in fact we have accommodated His will to our own inclinations. The next step in such a process is to identify that accommodation with the external form of demand—the Ten Commandments, for example—and lay claim to adherence to those commandments. We can claim such an accomplishment only if we forget that, as the scripture says, those commandments are "exceedingly broad" (Psalm 119:96), if we forget that through them we are dealing with the livng God, who is never satisfied with us as we are, but who always calls us to higher things. He is easy to please, but hard to satisfy. That was what our Lord intended to portray when he related the parable of the pearl and when he counseled the rich young ruler. The gift is freely given, but it demands no less than all. And the all that we give is really nothing, emptiness. Only the individual of genuine faith can know this.

What is it that we are obedient *to*? There are different ways of putting the answer to this question. I say *the* answer because I believe that there is only one. Christians say that their discipleship consists in obedience to God as He has made Himself known in Jesus Christ. That is the nub of the matter. Nonetheless, in answering the question, Christians speak in different ways. They sometimes speak of the *demand,* sometimes of the *call,* sometimes of the *vision.*

The *demand* is like that which a master makes of his servant. The personal analogy is here preserved. There is always a tendency toward legalism, however, if the demand is identified with a set of laws. When that shift of emphasis occurs, there is always the risk of believing that it is within our grasp to fulfill the demand by performing the prescribed deeds or by refraining from the proscribed deeds. But the demand is the impossible possibility.

The *call* is to a life. Christians may speak of the call at the beginning of their life of faith, if they find that there was a time when their faith had a particular beginning. But we should not think of the call as referring only to a beginning. God calls us to a life of continual response. The call continues as long as life shall last.

Paul spoke of his obedience to the *vision.* " 'I was not,' " he said, " 'disobedient to the heavenly vision' " (Acts 26:19). The demand of the vision did not cease. He had seen the resurrected Christ, and then and there the vision that he saw placed upon him a responsibility which he would never escape. He often recalled that vision and responded to its demand as he pressed on in the work to which it urged him.

The beginning of faith is the beginning of obedience. The continuing of faith is the continuing of obedience. Faith and obedience are a unity. We should not think that faith comes first and that the obedience follows. It is wrong to think of faith and obedience in terms of *now* and *then*. *Now* you have faith, and *then* you will be obedient. There cannot be faith without obedience. Nor can there be obedience without faith. Faith is the condition of obedience, and obedience is the condition of faith. Only he who believes is obedient, and only he who is obedient believes.

Questions

1. What is legalism?
2. Define antinomianism.
3. How may both extremes be avoided?
4. Explain the apparent contradiction in the following texts: "The law is not of faith" (Galatians 3:12, K.J.V.). "Do we then make void the law through faith? God forbid: yea, we establish the law" (Romans 3:31, K.J.V.).

Chapter 10

Christian Sanctification

Scripture sets before us the challenge to perfection in two imperatives: " 'Be perfect' " and " 'Have faith in God.' " Should we tend to become self-satisfied in our faith, it reminds us to " 'be perfect.' " It is very easy to accommodate ourselves to what we have become. Christians should know what God expects from the life of faith. Christian perfection is not absolute perfection. Nor is it something unattainable by the ordinary believer. What, then, is it?

We first must recognize that we are sinners. We are the kind of people who do particular sins. Recognition of our condition is an essential ingredient in Christian sanctification.

Whatever perfection we have is accomplished in our human nature. We do not have to be transformed into little deities in order to be perfect. We are sanctified in our humanity.

Perfection is the "natural" condition of Christians. As the body has a normal way of dealing with pain, so faith has a way of dealing with sin.

The New Testament clearly states that we are to be perfect. It also asserts that as Christians we sin and we need forgiveness. We are to be perfect, but we need forgiveness. That is the antithesis, and Scripture does not seek to resolve it. Believers in this condition are called saints.

Paul's correspondence with the church at Corinth illustrates this. He addresses the Corinthian believers (in spite of all their faults) as "saints," or "sanctified" ones. Why? Because they had come to believe in God through Jesus Christ?

So the need for faith becomes central. There may not always be the desired explanation, and this makes intellectual doubt always possible. Not all our questions have to be answered. But that does not matter. Faith and life are not rewards for smartness.

The call for faith is thus the call for perfection. Those who are sanctified continue in the faith, by which they know that God accepted them.

In the course of his Sermon on the Mount Jesus said: " 'You, therefore, must be perfect' " (Matthew 5:48). Later, after having performed the unusual act of cursing the fig tree and making it wither, He instructed His disciples: " 'Have faith in God' " (Mark 11:22).

The Christian life is one of movement. It is not static but dynamic. For life itself is such. We move through change to new situations. Different situations challenge us to make old decisions in a new way. To halt is to die. The resources of the whole personality are touched by the movement of the Christian life: the will, the emotions, the intellect. The entire being is subject to the call of Christ to discipleship.

Our texts for this chapter give the imperatives. But are both injunctions necessary? Cannot the Christian life be summed up in one and one only? Why are these two imperatives to be placed side by side in the life of the Christian? Both imperatives, together, express the dialectic of Christian living. When we are apt to become self-satisfied with our spiritual condition and wish to maintain the status quo, the command comes: " 'You, therefore, must be perfect.' " It is a word to arouse us to self-examination and to diligence. On the other hand, occasions arise when we are about to despair over our failures. At such times we are tempted to call into question the purpose of Christian discipleship. But in our faltering, the other word comes to us: " 'Have faith in God.' " We never outgrow the need to have both words spoken to us.

The words of Jesus urge us to " 'be perfect' " when we are apt to forget that the Christian life entails denial, sacrifice, and effort. The word comes to us at those times when we are ready to think that we, to some extent or other, have attained a position of favor with God. " 'Be perfect' " is a command spoken to us in our moral self-sufficiency, when we are apt to say, "I have kept the rules. I am thankful that I am not as other people are." Jesus addresses the same words to us in our intellectual self-sufficiency, when we are apt to say, "I know the truth. I have mastered the tradition. I am thankful that I am not as others are." It counters a security of our own making and a contentment with our mediocrity. Through it Jesus opposes our spiritual laziness, our "solafidian sloth." We must be perfect with the more exceeding righteousness that God gives to us.

Surely, this is a very necessary word, one which, in the condition of our mortality, we shall never outgrow the need to hear. But what does it mean?

What do we expect from the Christian life? Do we expect—we shall use the expression for the moment—too much? Then when we do not get what we expect, are we frustrated and discouraged, bewildered and anxious? Do we expect too little? Then, for another reason, do we become discouraged by defeat or by the gnawing sense that there is more to fulfillment in Christian discipleship than what we have known? What, then, do we expect from the Christian life? In what terms are we to talk about what we might expect? If we can see the target, we shall have something to aim at. If we know the road, we shall be able to direct ourselves in the right path and not, like Don Quixote, go galloping off in all directions at once.

The words of Jesus tell us what we should expect: "'You, therefore, must be perfect.'" I am convinced that one of the reasons why there is not more vitality in Christian discipleship on the part of most believers is at least in part that they are not clear as to what they may expect from the Christian life. So the question "What do we expect from the Christian life?" becomes of great importance.

Now, if you were a housewife who had just received an ultramodern cooker, you would immediately want to find out what you could expect that cooker to do for you. You would try to ascertain its functioning capabilities. But that would not be enough. It is one thing to know what you must do to operate it efficiently, but also you will have to put it to use so that you can get out of it what could be expected. There is both the knowing and the doing. This is true in human relationships, also. To know what another competent person is capable of doing and to get him to do it on a certain occasion are by no means the same thing! Most people have hidden resources and capacities and affections awaiting release. It is important, then, to know what to expect.

Suppose that you have to drive through a city for the first time. Various options are open to you. You can stop at every other filling station, get a series of "can't miss it" directions, and trust that you will not miss any of the landmarks. Or you may simply drive on and on and hope to muddle through. Or you might consult a map and get some foreknowledge of what to expect. Then, even if you meet the unexpected (one-way traffic, diversions, or other such "motoring joys"), you will have a sense of direction and know where you are going. You will be able to take the diversions in your stride.

What, then, is the Christian to expect? A passage from the book of Hebrews says: "Strive for . . . the holiness without which no one will see the Lord" (chapter 12:14). What is holiness? The terms *holiness, perfection,* and *sanctification* are synonyms. To what reality do they point?

We may begin to understand if first we make two denials. (One way of making clear what something is, is to set out a denial of what it is not. Then one has prepared the way to say what it is.) Perfection for the believing Christian is not absolute perfection. This belongs to God alone. Whatever is creature is imperfect in relation to the absolute perfection of the divine. Nor is Christian perfection a lofty, abstract ideal that is open only to those who possess a certain kind of competence or who seclude themselves to a certain way of life that is not for most individuals. Perfection does not presuppose a kind of Gnostic esotericism or any kind of solitary asceticism. In setting out positively what these two denials intend, we must say, then: God gives us whatever perfection we have. It is derived. He imparts it by His grace. Furthermore, Christian perfection is for everyone. Anyone who believes may be perfect.

What, then, is perfection, or sanctification? It is a state in which progress is being made. That state is the state of faith. Faith is not static. It implies dynamic movement, "from faith to faith" (Romans 1:17, K.J.V.).

Now we can describe perfection in three affirmations.

1. The first element in Christian perfection is recognizing that we are sinners. This is first in importance. We never get to the place, progress as we may by God's grace, where we leave behind us the consciousness that we are sinners. This does not simply mean that we recognize that we have done sinful acts *a* and *b* and *c* and *d*. It is a much more profound recognition than this. It means acknowledging that we are the kind of people who do such things. Sin is not a problem that can be handled by patching up a sin here and a sin there. Instead, the spring of sins must be stopped. To recognize that we are sinners means that we recognize there is a power that lords it over us and prevents us from being what God intends us to be. That power is the power of *sin*. The sin within us gives rise to sins without. The individual acts of sinning issue from the underlying sin that dominates me. Those individual acts of sin are done by me, the sinner.

2. Whatever perfection is ours is accomplished in our *human nature*. God does not change us into little gods before we become holy. Our perfection is appropriate to our humanity. It is relative to our humanity. But it is not relative in the sense that it is insufficient. What God gives is never insufficient. God gives us perfection, as He gives us faith. To put it in other terms, God gives what He requires.

So it is not a perfection that we could manufacture for ourselves. The only perfection that we could make for ourselves would be a legal, external perfection, which would never come within a universe of faith. We could be perfect if we set up the standard ourselves. A boy could write a perfect exam paper, theoretically! One could make a perfect model. But what of a perfection that goes beyond our human capacities but that must yet be realized in our humanity? That would be beyond us. But God demands it of us. "'You, therefore, must be perfect.'" A perfection beyond our capacity and nature would be a useless demand unless it was possible to have it given to us, to receive it from without ourselves. This is what the Bible teaches us. God sanctifies our *humanity*. There is no other sanctification. We must be able to say—even if we might hesitate: "Unless I am sanctified now, I never will be."

3. Perfection is the "natural" condition of the Christian. As health is the natural condition of the body, so sanctification is the natural condition of the believer. It is not natural for us to complain of a pain here, and a pain there, and a pain somewhere else if we are healthy. Nor is it natural for the believer to be constantly having to recognize, "Oh, I did wrong again" and "Oh, I fell again." It is not that Christians do not sin, any more than that the body does not have pain. Just as the natural physical body has a way of dealing with pain, so faith has a way of dealing with unfaith. It is not exceptional, but normal, for Christians to be holy, perfect.

Jesus' command to be perfect does not stand alone in the New Testament. There are other similar commands. "Let us cleanse ourselves from every defilement of body and spirit, and make holiness perfect in the fear of God" (2 Corinthians 7:1). "Strive for . . . the holiness without which no one will see the Lord" (Hebrews 12:14).

On the other hand, Scripture explicitly recognizes that Christians will sin and will need forgiveness, and needing it, shall receive it. "If we say we have no sin, we deceive ourselves, and the truth is not in us. If we confess our sins, he is faithful and just, and will forgive our sins and cleanse us from all unrighteousness. If we say we have not sinned, we make him a liar, and his word is not in us" (1 John 1:8-10). "Wretched man that I am! Who will deliver me from this body of death? Thanks be to God through Jesus Christ our Lord! So then, I of myself serve the law of God with my mind, but with my flesh I serve the law of sin. There is therefore now no condemnation for those who are in Christ Jesus" (Romans 7:24-8:1).

We are to be perfect. But we sin. We are to be perfect. But we need forgiveness. The New Testament writers realistically recognized and portrayed our situation. It is in this ambiguous situation that we, the believers, are called "saints" *(hagioi)*, as for example in 1 Corinthians 1:2, and sixty-six other times in the New

Testament.*

We can now define *sanctification.* It is a state of acceptance with God in which, despite our sin, we progress in the life of faith. It is the state of faith. So every Christian is a saint.

But Scripture uses another word—the word *teleios;* and it is used quite frequently in the New Testament. It means complete, mature, having reached a goal or a stage, perfect. It has a range of meanings that makes it rather more concrete than the English word *perfect,* which requires explanation before you really know what it means.

The word *teleios* answers the question "What ought a person to be?" The perspective is forward-looking. The writers of the New Testament set our sights on what we may be, not on what we already are. We are to grow, and there is a perfection, or maturity, appropriate to each stage of growth. Paul urged his readers on to a perfection that they had not reached. He encouraged them to press ahead, like the runner competing in the games. The more perfect Christians are, the more they press ahead for the prize. (See Philippians 3:12-16.)

Sometimes the word *perfect* refers to the mind. The mind is renewed and exemplifies "what is good and acceptable and perfect" (Romans 12:2). The term *perfect* may be used, thus, to designate those who strive for mastery, for progress, who look forward to the possibilities of Christian development. "Let those of us who are perfect [*teleioi*] think in this way," or as the Revised Standard Version renders it, "Let those of us who are mature be thus minded (Philippians 3:15). Epaphras prayed that the church at Colossae would "stand perfect" (Colossians 4:12, K.J.V.).

The Epistle to the Hebrews (in chapters 5 and 6) complains that the readers are like babies, whereas they should be *teleioi,* mature. They cannot take the "solid food" that is for the perfect. They ought to be able to pass from the "elementary doctrines" and go on to perfection. They ought to be mature enough to take new and advanced teachings, and not have the old matters constantly repeated to them as though they had never heard them before.

John in his Epistles rebuked his readers for thinking that they were sinless (see 1 John 2:1-4). He was speaking about love. Love

---

* C. Ryder Smith (*The Biblical Doctrine of Man*, p. 191) counted sixty-seven usages of *hagioi* in the New Testament.

is the atmosphere in which the disciples move. God's love is revealed in Jesus Christ. The Christians respond by loving God and loving their fellows. Love for God is perfected for one who keeps the word of Christ (verse 5). The love of God is perfected in us "if we love one another" (chapter 4:12). Perfection is possible through Christ. Christ can make the believers perfect. Their perfection will grow as they abide in Him.

"The New Testament writers never refer to Christians who *are* perfect in any *final* sense. Still less does any Christian in that book claim any such perfection. How could he when he thought of Jesus? None, indeed, claims even a relative perfection. . . . The Apostolic writers show no interest in the question: 'Are there any perfect men?' Their uniform message is, 'By the grace of Christ go forward!' Nonetheless they never suggest that Christ *cannot* make a man all that he ought to be." [18]

Paul in his letter to the Corinthian believers begins by calling them saints. But what a church! First Corinthians is one long rebuke of fault after fault. The saints were partisan. Their factions had split the church into half a dozen parties, so they could not hear the gospel when it was preached. One brother was living with his father's wife. One member was going against another in a pagan court of law, yet coming to the same place of worship. Then there were those rich saints who would become drunk at the church assemblies, while the poor received no consideration whatsoever. The saints at Corinth spoke in jibberish, and such was the confusion at the meetings of worship that Paul agreed that a pagan entering the gathering would conclude that they were mad. They had no real understanding of the resurrection. Paul had to correct them, point by point, upon its reality and meaning. Yet, to use Paul's own term, they were the "saints" that were "at Corinth."

Was there any difference between them and non-Christians? Paul thought so. He said so. After having listed some of the sins common in the society of the day (some of which were still evident within the Corinthian church), he added: "And such were some of you. But you were washed, you were sanctified, you were justified in the name of the Lord Jesus Christ and in the Spirit of our God" (chapter 6:11). There was a difference. Faith had made the difference: faith in the resurrected Christ. The Corinthians were sinful and sinning deeply, but the important thing was that they believed. They had been justified. They were sanctified. They had faith. That made the difference! But they had a long way to go.

Their holiness was to be perfected (2 Corinthians 7:1). The presence and the persistence of faith within their midst guaranteed that they would be perfected. The saints were making progress.

We may say, then, that Christians are holy as they have faith in Jesus as Lord. They maintain their faith that God has saved them in Jesus Christ. That is sanctification. "The fundamental doctrine is that Christians are 'holy' because, through Christ by the Spirit, they are *in fellowship* with God, and therefore, in their small and imperfect way, *like* him."[19]

We are holy. We are perfect as we have faith in Jesus Christ. We do not have to worry about our past sins, for God has taken care of that burden. We do not have to worry about our future progress and perfection, for they too are in God's hands. We do have to manifest faith here and now. As we have such faith, God looks at us through Jesus Christ—as perfect. We are at the same time sinner and righteous. "[God] takes us at the same time for sinners and nonsinners. Sin remains and simultaneously does not remain in us."[20]

The term *sanctification* describes one who really believes. It describes the one who is justified by faith. It is the description of those who have come to trust God, who can accept their limitations and responsibilities, and who have come to live life from a new center. A new principle guides them.

These people have changed their citizenship. (See Hebrews 11:14-16.) "We . . . are citizens of heaven" (Philippians 3:20, N.E.B). This is an instructive figure. The process of becoming the citizen of another country is a long one. One must accommodate oneself to the customs of the new country, perhaps even learn a new language. But a time comes when the acclimatization is complete, which may or may not coincide with the receipt of naturalization papers. So with the life of faith. There is a process of acclimatization to another world, to another age, to another country. A new motif permeates the life. New motives become dominant. It is not that we are given a new status; rather, a new life is conferred and becomes reality within us, expressing itself in conduct.

Love becomes the animating principle of life. Old things pass away under the influence of the expulsive power of a new affection. Not, it is to be noted, under the compulsive power of a new law. If we live by rule, we shall find ourselves in situations that the rules do not cover, and if there is no one to make a new rule for us, what then? Rules will fail us—at the very time we need them most. No one can legislate the love of the heart by which we are to live.

Perfection means that we live the life of faith and that we see our sin through our faith. We shall have to live with our sin. But we may live with sin in one of two ways: either as forgiven or as unforgiven. If we live with it, taking sin for granted as a normal matter, then failure will become a matter of course. The Christian can never rest content with failure. To do so, in any respect, signifies the stagnation of faith, which must then be revitalized.

We must now turn to Jesus' other command: " 'Have faith in God' " (Mark 11:22). We never get to the place where this command is irrelevant. When it is a question of submitting to the call of discipleship, " 'Follow me,' " it is the demand for faith. When it is a question of maintaining the fellowship with God in Jesus Christ, when it is assailed by sin, it is the call to faith. God reveals; we respond in faith. God calls us to a life of discipleship. " 'Have faith,' " He says. We may say to the person whose zeal is flagging and whose courage is low, "Have faith in God"; to him who is hard pressed as a Christian in the battle against sin, "Have faith in God"; to him who is perplexed with doubt, "Have faith in God." It is never inappropriate to set forth the command, " 'Have faith in God.' " It is the watchword of the Christian religion.

I mentioned doubt. Wherever there is doubt, we may call for faith. But there is also doubt about doubt, so we need to address ourselves to the doubter. Who is the doubter who needs to be called to faith? Every doubter needs to be called to faith. And we have all doubted.

Now, doubt is of various kinds, and we must distinguish *intellectual* doubt from *experiential* doubt. We may be puzzled about the existence of God, for example, because someone has raised some questions in our minds. But we may also be puzzled about the existence of God because we have watched a loved one suffer long weeks of pain, only to be terminated by death.

Intellectual doubt comes when problems are raised with reference to what we thought was perfectly clear and simple. Can such doubts threaten faith? May doubt about the particular formulation of a doctrine involve repudiating one's faith in Jesus as the Christ? At what point, if at any, do intellectual doubts threaten faith? Note that one does not have to be an intellectual to understand what is meant by this kind of doubt. Doubt is by no means the sin of the sophisticated. One can doubt very simply!

Consider, for example, those young people standing at the

threshold of life. They are about to leave the protected atmosphere of home and local church, for they are driven to seek their own answers, to live life upon their own resources, and to live it in a secular world that questions their basic presuppositions. These young people have little idea of the threats that can be brought against faith and the persuasive appeals of non-Christian ideology. Besides, it is easy to absorb that which we have never been conditioned to resist or to recognize.

We have witnessed and shall witness more and more in the days to come, young people reared in Christian homes facing the impact of non-Christian ways of thinking. They have had to face the question of whether they should retain or abandon faith itself. Often they have wrestled with doubt concerning the reality of faith and the meaning of the realities confessed to be the objects of faith. The day is past when clear-minded youth will be satisifed with assertions made on the basis of authority. To neglect the dimensions of this problem is to ask for more and more defections. I do not refer to those who doubt everything on principle or to those who will never doubt anything. I speak of those who are genuinely perplexed by real and genuine questions, yet who desire to continue to be Christian. As a teacher of theology I find that both of the former are really dishonest, but the latter are honest souls who desperately need help.

The Christian college and university should provide the atmosphere within which there can be a sympathetic handling of intellectual problems, within the context of faith, so that students may come to Christian maturity and be prepared for the secularism of the age they have to face. This is the vocation of the Christian teacher.

Religious faith is put to the test in many ways *that can be anticipated*, when we speak of the possibility of intellectual doubt. Preparation can thus be made for such tests. A center of learning is concerned with intellectual matters. A Christian center of learning is concerned with those areas where it is appropriate to suggest interpretations that are either required or suggested by the fact of Christian faith. But I must be clear on one point: For some problems there are no *distinctively* Christian answers or methods of approach. For instance, each science has its own methodology—that is what makes it that particular science. There is no such thing as Presbyterian geometry, Baptist physics, or Adventist biology.

There will always be questions, of course. Some of us have

spent most of our lives considering the best ways to approach certain questions. There will also always be faith. Faith in God through Jesus Christ does not depend upon the answers to puzzling intellectual questions. If it did, only the smart and the brilliant would have faith. Christian faith is of a different order. Not all our questions will be answered. Not all our doubts will be resolved. But that does not matter. What ultimately matters is that faith be present everywhere, providing the atmosphere for the exercise of the intellect about those matters that puzzle it. " 'Have faith in God' "—even in the face of intellectual doubt.

Then there is experiential doubt. Once again the invitation is appropriate: " 'Have faith in God.' " No one who has stood beside the grave of a loved one or who has suffered at great length, witnessed suffering, or thought about suffering can fail to ask, "Where is God? Is there anybody there?" It is with this sensitivity to the ills of the world that the demand becomes acute, "Have faith! Do not abandon faith." It is then that the decision is made. Have faith in God! Suffering and the experiential doubt that accompanies it may be a means to faith. Have faith in God!

The call to faith is the call to perfection. These are not, in fact, two calls, but one. The demand that we be perfect is none other than the call to repose ourselves upon Jesus as the revelation of God.

Furthermore, the call to faith is a present call. It may not be deferred. Whatever teaches us to defer our faith relationship and its consequent challenge is a dangerous heresy that we must strenuously oppose. It is a second-chance doctrine. We may plead, "Let me go on, at least just this once." Just this once? And then? What will we be saying after tomorrow? How many more tomorrows do we need? This is the cry of a half-sensitive conscience or a resisting will. If someone offered you a million dollars, how long would it take you to be rich? It is not a matter of time; it is a matter of acceptance, of willingness.

We are saved by grace, and grace is costly. It is humbling to take what we had tried to get by our own efforts. We have to be shattered at the very core of our proud personality before we can even begin to live the life we were made for.

Grace will cost all that we have, for if we hang on to anything we will be hanging on to sin. Grace costs. The gift is freely given, but it is given to the humble: to the one whose defenses have been penetrated, whose hands are raised in surrender high above his head, whose knees are bent. We must stoop before He conquers.

There is a compulsion about this grace. First the compulsion to submit, and then the compulsion to live life under the cross—and that takes all there is. This gift costs all there is of us. God freely gives, but He demands no less than all.

Faith is a living, active, obedient faith. In the words of Dietrich Bonhoeffer: *"Only he who believes is obedient, and only he who is obedient believes."*[21] Our obedience is made real in the humdrum, rough-and-tumble, dog-eat-dog world of daily existence. Jesus invited, " 'Follow me' " (Mark 2:14). Paul urged, "Let this mind be in you, which was also in Christ Jesus" (Philippians 2:5, K.J.V.) and, also, "Yield your members to righteousness for sanctification" (Romans 6:19).

Questions

1. What is a saint?
2. How would you explain the meaning of the term *sanctification*?
3. Would you accept the expression "Sanctification by faith alone"? Explain.

Chapter 11

The Assurance of Faith

How can I know that my faith is in God? The doctrine of assurance is an essential Protestant doctrine. Along with God's gift of forgiveness comes the knowledge of that forgiveness. We know that we have been forgiven. Like the experience of trusting someone, it brings an immediate certainty that requires no further appeal. The certainty of God's love is not one into which we are argued by a process of proof. The assurance of salvation is a gift of God's grace. It is the witness of the Spirit. We know we have been accepted.

We should distinguish between two kinds of doubt. On the one hand is radical doubt. It questions the reality of God's presence and quenches faith. On the other hand is doubt about how we are to understand. Because we are human, our understandings are always only partial. There will always be the possibility of fresh light and clearer vision.

In Jesus Christ we come to know the demand of a holy God and the perverseness of a sinful will. God's revelation does not consist in the mere passing on of information, but in His coming to man with His demand and with His gift.

With the coming of Christian faith comes also the possibility of Christian explanations. New perspectives and interpretations become possible. Christian theology becomes possible.

With the coming of Christian faith is also the creation of the Christian Scriptures. The New Testament burns with the conviction that through the man Jesus, God has come. The Scriptures were written to bear witness of Him. The New Testament emphatically places Jesus Christ, the source of the reality of reconciliation, at the center. Without faith in him, the books of the New Testament would never have been.

As the apostles spoke their witness, the God who was among them in Jesus came powerfully again. So with the Written Word. As God comes to us through the Spirit when we read these words, we are led to Him by their instrumentality.

In this way the assurance of the knowledge of God is mediated and nurtured.

How can I know that my faith is in God? It seems a reasonable question, and so we shall address ourselves to it. One can answer this question in three ways. First, one can insist that we cannot know. We are never sure that our faith is in God. Second, others affirm that we may have *reasonable* surety. Since surety is always mixed with doubt, however, we can never be absolutely certain. Third, some Christians answer that in faith we may be assured beyond doubt of the knowledge of God and of our reconciliation with God.

All of us find it very hard to live with uncertainty about the things that really matter. Assured knowledge of the fulfillment of our basic needs seems to us to be a necessity. We could never rest content with a probable knowledge of the love of those whom we hold most dear. We must know for certain. Our security depends upon our knowing for sure that we can rely upon the other's word or the other's love. For many people, life is simply a quest for security. We seek to know certain things for sure.

No wonder it is important to ask whether we can be certain of faith. And it is here that we make contact with our Protestant heritage, which has as one of its sources the quest for certainty, a quest that was satisfied in the assurance that faith experienced. The doctrine of assurance is an essential Protestant Christian doctrine.

We know that our faith is directed aright because we know that we have been reconciled to God. The Christian experience of forgiveness gives us the direct assurance that faith is valid. We *know* that we have been forgiven, and this assurance does not require some other kind of support to validate it.

When I say that I trust someone, the one thing I am certain about is my knowledge of that trust. I would say, "I am certain that I trust John." That certainty is like the certainty we express when we say, "I am certain that I am forgiven." We do not have to appeal away from it to something else. It is an immediate deliverance of our experience. It does not need a further check. And just as there is no answer to the objector who says, "No, you do not trust John," so there is no answer to the objector who says, "No, your sins are not forgiven." In order for you to know what I know, you must have a similar experience.

What, then, does the Protestant teaching of assurance mean? We may make this clear by considering the following incident. "As Pope Gregory the Great put it, with the bland arrogance of all paternalism: *Sancta ecclesia fidelibus suis . . . spem miscet et metum.* (Holy Church mingles hope and fear for her faithful children.) Replying to one of the ladies-in-waiting at the Imperial Court, who had written to him for assurance, the great pope replied: *Secura de peccatis tuis fieri non debes.* (Thou shouldest not become easy in mind about thy sins.) In one sense, this is unexceptionable theology; such a warning bears witness to a true and inescapable element in that paradoxical doctrine of Assurance which the Reformers rediscovered in the New Testament. . . . But, to use an exact though crude metaphor, the medieval Church came to trade on this insecurity; the whole degrading trade in Indulgences which became a moral outrage in the early sixteenth century, shows that the scrupulous Catholic did not know and might not know on what terms he stood, so to speak, with God. Luther felt that he must know."[22]

The Protestant doctrine of assurance means that believers may know that their sins have been forgiven and that God has accepted them. Christians do not have to be in constant doubt. They need not fear that God's acceptance is not a reality. They may know for a certainty that they have been reconciled to God. This assurance does not have to depend upon some external forms or proofs. It is a certainty given by God Himself and known in the experience of reconciliation itself. Along with the acceptance, God also gives the assurance of that acceptance.

God's forgiveness is not provisional. He gives it freely. It is complete. It does not depend upon our goodness. Like that of the father in the parable of the prodigal son, God's forgiveness is free, undeserved, and unqualified. Only so can we be sure that it is real. If assurance depended either upon our goodness or upon something that we could do, we could never know it as a continuous and permanent characteristic of the life of faith. If our assurance depended upon future performance, it would be a phantom. When God forgives, His forgiveness is both free and real. It is not provisional.

"This notion, that when God forgives the sinful what He actually does is not to take them back to His heart, freely and unreservedly, but to take them on trial, is I think, manifestly out of touch with so central a part of Jesus' teaching as the Parable of the Prodigal. . . . Provisional pardon is an idea scarcely fitted to evoke a joy unspeakable and full of glory, or to inspire the tempted with unwavering courage."[23]

As the pardon and the acceptance of God is full and free, so the assurance of that acceptance may be certain and constant. Thus we may have courage in the hour of testing, and fortitude in times of opposition. God has received us. His pardon is complete. Since the Father's pardon is complete, the believer's joy may be also. There is music and feasting and abiding relief.

The object of Christian faith is God, the gracious God who has manifested His loving will in Jesus Christ. Now, faith is shaped by its Object. It is not formed by human works. It takes its character from what is revealed through it. Therefore, because we have come to know God we can speak of the assurance of faith. The Object of our faith is the ultimate of all realities. The certainty of faith is the most secure of all assurances.

Only those who have experienced this reality can speak of it as it should be spoken of. Only believers can testify to the assurance of faith. To nonbelievers it appears odd, even irrational. "The love of Jesus—what it is, None but His loved ones know." [24] There can be no question of rational proof, any more than we may speak of rational proof for the certainty of another's love. If we are not certain at the outset, no lesser certainties can confirm the reality of such experiences. No one can argue me out of my certainty of God's love, because I am not argued into it. Reason has its place, but its place is not here. Reason comes after faith and explicates it. Reason can never establish faith. To confuse knowledge and faith is Gnosticism, a temptation that has always lured the church. But salvation is not the reward for intelligence. It is the gift of grace for all.

Similarly, the salvation of human beings does not rest upon how we feel, but upon what God has done. And the assurance of salvation is likewise dependent upon God's act within the believers. Christians call this act "the witness of the Spirit." So the apostle wrote: "The Spirit itself beareth witness with our spirit, that we are the children of God" (Romans 8:16, K.J.V.). Paul here confesses that the certainty of his acceptance with God is not one that he gave himself. It came to him from God Himself. The God who was revealed in the manhood of Jesus was revealed within the apostle's experience.

The God who came in Jesus is manifest in the Spirit and gives assurance that the Saviour's work has been effective. God provides Christians with an inward certainty that He has accepted them and forgiven them. God's grace completes its outflow, so to speak, by giving to believers the assurance of its presence. In faith we are forgiven and receive the knowledge that forgiveness has come from God. Not only does God accept us but also He grants to us the knowledge that we have been accepted.

Acceptance with God is a relationship that we enter with God, whose will toward us is constant. Once accepted by God, we can rely upon the constancy of the eternal God and His continuing grace. Men and women of faith do not need to waver in this conviction of God's changelessness.

It is very important that we distinguish between two kinds of doubt. On the one hand, there is radical doubt. It calls into question the reality of the presence of God to humanity. This doubt undercuts Christian experience by denying its foundation in God's grace. To harbor this kind of doubt is to pass from faith to skepticism. When it comes to stay, the light of faith goes out.

On the other hand, there is the doubt of those who continue to affirm their faith and acceptance. They hear God's word, but they do not always see clearly what it means. None of us can always explain the meaning of what we know in experience, and so we may even call into question an explanation that we once embraced. Understanding grows, and there can never be growth in Christian understanding without the intervention of doubt. We must not think that because we are puzzled and unhappy about some doctrinal explanation that our experience of our Lord's acceptance is in jeopardy. It is true, of course, that serious theological misunderstandings can dry up faith or distort it. The Christian church has always warned of heresy and has drawn guidelines that, if followed, would direct discussion in the right paths. But, while recognizing the danger of misinterpretation and wrong emphasis in explanation, we must also recognize that our knowledge is only partial. We see through a glass darkly. Our insights are broken and fragmentary. There will always be room for bewilderment. But we must not think that our puzzlement indicates God's withdrawal. It may signify His presence. We must wait and see.

Thus understanding leads us to speak more specifically of the kind of knowledge that we have in the assurance of our acceptance. Faith has its source in God's grace. This grace has been revealed to us in Jesus Christ. This revelation of grace is for our reconciliation, not for our information. God reveals Himself to us not to convey knowledge but to save us from our lost condition.

So if we ask what we come to know in Jesus Christ, the answer is God and ourselves. Jesus reveals not merely additional information about the universe. The kind of knowledge we come to know through Him is not cosmological, scientific, or historical. Instead, we come to know the demand of a holy God and the reality of a sinful will that is bent away from God. The revelation of a gracious God does not consist in the mere passing on of information. It consists in His coming to us with His demand and with His gift.

This does not mean that Christians must set aside reason and intelligent discourse. When faith is present it makes possible new perspectives upon the world. It opens up new possibilities of interpretation in many dimensions. We see the world differently. We view history and philosophy differently. With the presence of Christ and the Christian's faith in him come answers to previously unanswered questions. With the presence of Christian faith comes also the possibility of Christian theology. Christian theology is the intelligent contemplation of God's revelation in Jesus Christ from the perspective of Christian faith.

The coming of Christian faith led to the creation of the Christian Scriptures. All the writers of the New Testament were men of faith. They had come to believe that Jesus is the Christ. They had found that in him God had come to them, and through him they had found forgiveness and reconciliation. It is to this acceptance that each, in his own way, bears testimony in his writing. The New Testament burns with one great conviction: Jesus is central for our knowledge of God. Through the man Jesus, God has come to us. The resurrection of Jesus from the dead marks the turning point in human history. God is present in victorious display. So one after the other they write that they are bearing witness to what they have known.

"That which was from the beginning, which we have heard, which we have seen with our eyes, which we have looked upon and touched with our hands, concerning the word of life—the life was made manifest, and we saw it, and testify to it, and proclaim to you the eternal life which was with the Father and was made manifest to us—that which we have seen and heard we proclaim also to you, so that you may have fellowship with us; and our fellowship is with the Father and with his Son Jesus Christ. And we are writing this that our joy may be complete" (1 John 1:1-4).

They wrote out their witness for a purpose. They did not write simply to inform. Rather, they sought to assist in the reader's coming to the faith they as writers knew: "Now Jesus did many other signs in the presence of the disciples, which are not written in this book; but these are written that you may believe that Jesus is the Christ, the Son of God, and that believing you may have life in his name" (John 20:30, 31).

Jesus' words in reference to the Old Testament are even more appropriate when applied to the New: " 'It is they that bear witness to me' " (chapter 5:39). The Scritures are witness. This sums it up. The purpose of Christian Scripture is to bear witness that God is decisively known in Jesus and that faith in him has brought reconciliation. The New Testament witnesses to what God has done in Jesus *for* us and what He has done and is doing through the Holy Spirit *in* us. The writers witness both to their faith and to Jesus, their lord, the source of that faith.

The inspired writers had experienced the reality of reconciliation. In the books that we now call the New Testament, they testify of that reality. But the Source of that reality is emphatically placed always at the center. God has come to us. The Word who is God has come to mankind in the flesh. "In the beginning was the Word, and the Word was with God, and the Word was God. He was in the beginning with God; all things were made through him, and without him was not anything made that was made." "And the Word became flesh and dwelt among us, full of grace and truth; we have beheld his glory, glory as of the only Son from the Father" (chapter 1:1-3, 14).

Jesus is the Word. God is the Word. The Word is manifest. Before there was a line of Christian Scripture, before there could be, God came to us in the flesh. Before there was the *spoken* word of Christian faith there was God the Word made flesh. Before there was the *Written* Word of Christian faith there was God the Word made flesh. Out of the matrix of the revelation of God the Word in the flesh have sprung those primary and irreplaceable documents of Christian faith, the books of the New Testament. Without faith they would never have been. Without Jesus, the Christ of faith would never have been. Indeed, to say "Jesus Christ" is to make confession of faith. The primary fact is the fact of Jesus Christ, the manifestation of God. It is the reality of the manifest presence of God in the world that gives to the Scriptures their unique authority.

So we return to our theme of the assurance of the Spirit. The New Testament writers knew that the cross was not the end. The resurrection followed the crucifixion. The coming of the Holy Spirit was the means of assuring them that the God who came to them in Jesus, as the Son who died, was indeed not absent from them now. Although He was not among them in the flesh, as Son, He was nevertheless present in powerful reality. No one less than God Himself could convict and bring the judgment of guilt upon sinners as the spoken word was preached. " 'And when he comes, he will convince the world concerning sin and righteousness and judgment' " (chapter 16:8).

What is true of the spoken word also holds true of the Written Word. It is as God comes to us through the reading of Scripture that we are led to God. The words of Scripture are then not merely lifeless words on a page, but they are the instrument through which the presence of the living God becomes a reality to us.

In speaking of the knowledge of faith, we must hold together both Scripture and Spirit. If we speak only of Scripture and forget the Spirit, we are in danger of an intellectualistic approach to Scripture that shows itself in an undue concern for the letter. If we speak only of the Spirit, we are in danger of subjectivism, for we may identify our desire or expectation or dogma with the deliverance of the Spirit.

Through the Spirit, the Written Word is the means through which God Himself comes to us. The Written Word mediates the Reality it announces. Like the sacraments, it does not simply remind us of a past, which for us may be dead. Rather, it reminds us of the past to mediate to us a Living Presence, in the present. The word that does not mediate to us the living presence of the speaker is not a genuinely living word. It has failed to communicate the essential. If it does not serve to mediate that to which it witnesses, it is only an empty sign. When we read Scripture, we ought always to pray for the living presence of the God of our Lord Jesus Christ. For this is how the assurance of the knowledge of God is mediated and nurtured.

Questions

1. What do we mean by "the witness of the Spirit"?
2. Why does the Christian speak of God in trinitarian terms?
3. State briefly how the Christian Scriptures came to be written.
4. Preaching is witness. Witness to what?
5. What is meant by the Protestant doctrine of assurance?

Chapter 12

The Rewards of Faith

God is self-sufficient. What we have and are He gives to us. How, then, can we give God anything? If we respond to His gift to us, it is quite inappropriate to expect a reward for having so responded. God can never pay us, since He is never in our debt. We may never speak of God *paying* a reward. The reward is a *gift* of His grace.

We must not evaluate our standing with God on the basis of the exterior fortunes of our present life. God's reward is not material prosperity.

Some rewards are like wages: so much received for so much done. Such wages are paid, not given. The Christian's reward, however, is given, not paid. It is a gift of God's grace. A gift can never be earned. Our works and God's gifts are qualitatively different. We have no claim on God on the basis of our works.

God's reward to the believer is the gift of communion with Himself. Such communion not even death can terminate. Our intimation of final rewards is to be found in the present experience of communion. The criterion is not length of service or amount of works or any other kind of merit claim, but whether we reflect genuine faith and love.

What is a reward? Why is a reward given? Is a reward a gift given or a debt paid? What is the nature of the Christian's reward?

The first thing that we must remember when we talk about the Christian's reward is that God is self-sufficient. He is the Creator. Whatever exists does so because He has willed it into being. All creatures have their being in God. In Him, and by virtue of His continued and continuing mercies, we have life and the means to continue living. All that we have is derived from the bounty of the all-sufficient Creator, who exists for His own sake. It is for His sake that we exist too. Humanity is thus utterly dependent upon God's providence for the blessings of life and its accompaniments.

Since all we are and have has its source in God's goodness, how can we give Him anything? How can we who have received everything from God act in any way as if we were giving Him anything? When a father receives a birthday gift from his child, he knows very well that he himself provided the means to buy the gift. But the act of giving nonetheless meaningfully expresses the child's mind and heart. But to expect a reward for having given father a gift that was bought with money which he supplied in the first place would be simply comical.

We sometimes speak of a reward being given for a certain amount of work done. The term, in this usage, simply means "payment." When the term *reward* has this sense, we can only deny it a place in our thinking about Christian faith. God can never pay us, since nothing we do can ever put Him in our debt. Whatever we receive is His gift to us. Thus we can never expect a reward from Him on the basis of our self-activity. Since God gives all (and one who is saved has received the gift), no one in this respect differs from anyone else. "For who sees anything different in you? What have you that you did not receive? If then you received it, why do you boast as if it were not a gift?" (1 Corinthians 4:7). Since God is the source of all that is, the Christian's reward is not earned and paid. The reward is given. Like faith, the reward is a gift of God's grace.

To recognize this is to avoid a common religious error. It is easy to assume that the prosperity of those who, according to certain standards, do well in life is because of their goodness. But then if the believer finds his lot hard and difficult and judges God's justice on such grounds, he is bound to become unhappy and discontented. Prosperity is no reward for faith. When we construe it as such, we place a wrong evaluation upon both prosperity and goods. Many a believer has begged bread, while the nonbeliever has reveled in affluence.

We must not look at matters in terms of a utilitarian interpretation of comfort and pain. Faith sees things differently. It perceives that no quantity of things and no prosperity can substitute for fellowship with God. Reward, from the point of view of faith, is not quantitative remuneration, but a quality of fellowship, which might very well require the removal of prosperity in order to persist. That is why a negative evaluation of suffering is inappropriate for the Christian believer. We should not measure fellowship with God by the presence or absence of goods.

Thus a transvaluation of values takes place. What by the standards of nonfaith is shunned, faith welcomes. What the hedonist welcomes, the believer regards as a danger. Christians must watch themselves very carefully in days of prosperity lest, in forgetting God as Lord, they be carried away by their many possessions and the comfort of the life they lead. Prosperity is not, in itself, an evidence of God's favor any more than poverty or suffering is an evidence of His disfavor. All of us stand before God in one of two categories: either as believers or as nonbelievers. What matters is the faith relationship of fellowship with God.

Nothing that we bring to God or do for Him can ever put Him in our debt. Nothing that we may enjoy or endure can ever, in itself, create or destroy faith in God and fellowship with Him. So, when speaking of rewards, we should avoid two errors. The first is the error of thinking that when God rewards us He is paying us for services rendered. The other is the parallel error of evaluating our standing with God on the basis of the exterior fortunes of our present life.

One day Sir Christopher Wren was walking around St. Paul's Cathedral while it was under construction. As he chatted with the various laborers, he asked one of them, "What are you working here for?"

"Ah, I must work somewhere, and building is as good a job as any, I suppose."

He turned to a second. "Why are you working here?"

"I've a wife and family to keep. I've got to earn money to maintain them."

But a third gave a different answer. "I'm helping Sir Christopher Wren build a cathedral!"

It is only natural to think of receiving a reward for labors done. That's the way the economic world looks at it. Quantitative remuneration holds the field for the workman. Because of his diligence a harder worker has more possibilities opened up before him. But there is work, and there are wages. As the one or the other is made prominent, the character of the work is affected. If I think constantly about the wages, I shall be mostly concerned about them. So long as I get them I am happy. In consequence my work suffers. If earning wages is the most important thing, I'll not be too worried about the work I do.

Fortunately, other laborers find a satisfaction in the work that they do. They are not concerned about the wages. Their reward is in their work. If that is accomplished well, they are happy. Have you watched a young boy make a snowman? The youngster is hot. His arms and legs ache. But he goes on with a gleeful smile because his heart is in his job. He knows something of the joy that comes to artist and poet who find all their satisfaction in their creative work. That reward is vastly greater than any mercenary rewards they could receive.

But what of Christians? What should be their attitude to final rewards? In their sermons what emphasis should Christian preachers place on rewards?

The idea of reward is certainly scriptural, but it is not one that the Biblical writers have thrust into the foreground. Romans 4:4 states a key principle: "Now to one who works, his wages are not reckoned as a gift but as his due." In other words, a person who works should receive wages, and the one for whom the work is done is in debt for the work done. What happens at the end of a busy week at the factory or shop or office? Employees receive their wages. When they receive their pay they do not go to the employer and overwhelm him with grateful thanks for their money. They know they have earned it. It is not a gift given, but a debt paid. However, we respond quite differently when we receive a gift, perhaps unexpectedly, from a friend. We do not just take it for granted and forget it. We take pains to render thanks for it. There is a great difference between a debt and a gift, even if they are identical in appearance.

The reward of the Christian is of grace, not of debt. It is a gift pure and simple. We have no right or merit by which we may claim any of the good things God gives us. We are sinful, and in obeying God we have only done our duty. On the basis of our obedience we can claim nothing. " 'Will any one of you, who has a servant plowing or keeping sheep, say to him when he has come in from the field, "Come at once and sit down at table"? Will he not rather say to him, "Prepare supper for me, and gird yourself and serve me, till I eat and drink; and afterward you shall eat and drink"? Does he thank the servant because he did what was commanded? So you also, when you have done all that is commanded you, say, "We are unworthy servants; we have only done what was our duty"' " (Luke 17:7-10).

The fulfillment of Christian duty affords no basis for claiming the reward. God's rewards are given. No performance of ours can put Him in our debt so that the reward is ours by dint of our labor or effort. "God doth not need either man's works or his own gifts."[25] When we have done all we should, we have no claim upon God. Were we to keep the whole law, our performance would be phenomenal, but it would not enable us to lay claim upon God's mercy. Our works and God's gifts are qualitatively different.

Furthermore, the Bible does not hold out rewards as bribes or inducements. It does not consider rewards compensation for losses or labors. The rewards come with the activity. Suppose a young man courts a young woman, wins her hand in marriage, and by so doing steps into a vast fortune. If he courted her merely to get her money, we would call him mercenary. After all, money is not the due reward for love. Happiness is. Love carries with it its own reward. So does the way of life that the Christian follows. C. S. Lewis observed that a proper reward is not something which has to be added on to the activity but is to be found in the activity itself, or in that to which the activity leads. A player immersed in his game, an artist absorbed in his creative work, find satisfaction enough in the doing of what they do. A general who fights for money rather than for victory is missing the mark. Victory is a general's reward.

On one occasion Jesus, referring to the ostentatious piety of Pharisees, observed: "'They have received their reward'" (Matthew 6:5). If we seek only for praise, we shall get only praise. If my motive is on a low plane, my reward will be also. If we want others to notice our spiritual exercises and vocations, we may very well receive their applause. But we shall get no more. Jesus' words indicate that we get the reward on the plane of our motive. The Greek expression Jesus used meant "they have been paid in full." There is nothing more.

Have you ever asked yourself: "Why am I a Christian? What lies behind my profession to follow Jesus as Lord? What motivates my good actions? Do I do good because I love Jesus? Do I find satisfaction purely in the good that I do?" We might sum up this series of questions by asking: What is the Christian's reward?

The reward is God's gift of Himself to the believer. It is the gift of communion as deep as the limitations of human existence can permit. It is a reward that is inherent in the life of faith and thus springs from it. It is a present award. In a word, the Christian's reward is satisfaction, and the highest satisfaction is found in the communion of faith. At last the quest is over. The wanderings have ended.

> Nor can the vain toil cease,
> Till in the shadowy maze of life we meet
> One who can guide our aching wayward feet
> To find Himself, our Way, our Life, our Peace!
> In Him the long unrest is soothed and stilled:
> Our hearts are filled!

Satisfaction in communion. That is the greatest reward that could be given, for God bestows it upon the consecrated and obedient who are consecrated and obedient without any thought of a reward.

But this is not all. Scripture also speaks about a time of future rewards. These will be an extension, and expansion, of those received on earth. They will be of the same species. Communion and satisfaction enhanced to infinity by the removal of all the barriers. " 'Blessed are you when men revile you and persecute you and utter all kinds of evil against you falsely on my account. Rejoice and be glad, for your reward is great in heaven, for so men persecuted the prophets who were before you' " (chapter 5:11, 12).

Jesus held out the promise of reward as a comfort to those who would suffer persecution. They do not get the reward because of the persecution. It is given in persecution. Love behind the endurance of the faithful finds its uninhibited atmosphere. The love for God that is stronger than death is not bound and terminated by death. Hence one may look beyond death to the consummation of the fellowship of faith in the life beyond.

"In him you also, who . . . have believed in him, were sealed with the promised Holy Spirit, which is the *guarantee* of our inheritance until we acquire possession of it" (Ephesians 1:13, 14; cf. 2 Corinthians 1:22; 5:5). Paul insists that our intimation of the future glory is a present fact in the fellowship with God given to us here and now. The best anticipation of future bliss is the present satisfaction of the believer.

Yes, the fundamental Christian teaching of salvation by faith does have a place for a doctrine of rewards. But we do not earn them. Instead, Scripture emphasizes a richer, deeper, and fuller life. And when we receive the last great reward, we shall receive in culmination that which we have already begun to experience in the limitations of human life. "For if these things are yours and abound, they keep you from being ineffective or unfruitful in the knowledge of our Lord Jesus Christ. . . . So there will be richly provided for you an entrance into the eternal kingdom of our Lord and Savior Jesus Christ" (2 Peter 1:8-11).

At times Jesus addressed the question What must I do so that I may *have*. . .? " 'What good deed must I do, to have eternal life?' " (Matthew 19:16), the rich young man asked Jesus. And Jesus pointed out that motive is more important than manner. It is not that certain acts insure certain results merely by the fact that they are performed. Jesus called into question the matter of regulating performance by a set of rules. Without the young man's willingness to give up everything for the sake of the kingdom, the performance of particular acts was of no avail. To him Jesus said, "If the performance of any of your acts is worthy, it will manifest itself in a willingness to abandon everything for my sake." The young man asked for more rules. Jesus demanded all that he had. "What is the motive?" Jesus asked the questioner.

Then in Matthew 20:1-16 we find the interesting parable of the laborers in the vineyard. Certain features of this parable lead one to conclude that Jesus meant to teach that it was *not* length of service that determined what the reward would be. If motive were not right, there could be no contentment.

Those with whom the owner had made a definite agreement grumbled at the end of the day. The master had stated only how much he would pay those who went to work at the beginning of the day. They had agreed to his offer. But when they saw others receiving the same reward as they received, they appealed to him on the grounds of length of service. But he did not consider their appeal valid. So it is with the matter of acceptance with God. It is not how long that matters. It does not even enter the question. Church membership for a quarter or half a century is not the issue. Nor is it how much that matters. There is no use in appealing to length of service or to the amount of work done. " 'On that day many will say to me, "Lord, Lord, did we not prophesy in your name, and cast out demons in your name, and do many mighty works in your name?" And then will I declare to them, "I never knew you; depart from me, you evildoers" ' " (chapter 7:22, 23).

According to the parable of the sheep and the goats, the rewards God bestows elicit genuine surprise both from the legalist ("Did not we do all kinds of things?") and from the righteous ("When did we do anything?") " 'Then the righteous will answer him, "Lord, when did we see thee hungry and feed thee, or thirsty and give thee drink? And when did we see thee a stranger and welcome thee, or naked and clothe thee? And when did we see thee sick or in prison and visit thee?" And the King will answer them, "Truly, I say to you, as you did it to one of the least of these my brethren, you did it to me" ' " (chapter 25:37-40).

What, then, should be our attitude to reward? We are not to think that it should be proportionate to the labors done. We are not to think we deserve any reward at all. We are not to look at it as the chief incentive. Instead, we should find joy in the very life that we live. In fact, in the Christian life of faith there is such present satisfaction that thought of reward always remains in the background. To love the Lord is to have confidence in His will.

We can question, then, our motives for engaging in certain acts of the Christian life. Why do we follow Christ? Why have we accepted Jesus' offer of salvation? Is it because we desire communion with the Divine? Why do we pray? Is prayer only request, or is it expression? Is prayer talk, or is it communion? Do we give because God promises to recompense us? Why do we keep the Sabbath? Is it because we have become so used to it that to change would disrupt a way of life that we do not want to alter?

"The precepts of the Lord are right, rejoicing the heart; the commandment of the Lord is pure, enlightening the eyes; the fear of the Lord is clean, enduring for ever; the ordinances of the Lord are true, and righteous altogether. More to be desired are they than gold, even much fine gold; sweeter also than honey and drippings of the honeycomb. Moreover by them is thy servant warned; in keeping them there is great reward" (Psalm 19:8-11).

That is the heart of the matter. Although all we do is unprofitable, yet in that very activity God speaks to us. Beyond this communion there is nothing more ultimate. The Christian loves the Lord for what He is and for what He has done. The following verse nicely summarizes the matter:

My God, I love Thee; not because
  I hope for heaven thereby,
Nor yet because who love Thee not
  Are lost eternally.

Thou, O my Jesus, Thou didst me
  Upon the cross embrace;
For me didst bear the nails, and spear,
  And manifold disgrace,

And griefs and torments numberless,
  And sweat of agony;
Yea, death itself; and all for me
  Who was thine enemy.

Then why, O blessèd Jesu Christ,
  Should I not love Thee well?
Not for the sake of winning heaven,
  Nor of escaping hell;

Not from the hope of gaining aught,
  Not seeking a reward;
But as Thyself hast loved me,
  O ever-loving Lord.

So would I love Thee, dearest Lord,
And in Thy praise will sing;

Solely because Thou art my God,
And my most loving King.[26]

Questions

1. State carefully what you understand by the word *reward.*
2. What is the nature of the Christian's reward? Is it given or paid, present or future?

Chapter 13

Offense or Faith?

Everyone responds in one of two possible ways with reference to Jesus: offense or faith. Coming to faith means having passed the possibility of offense.

Offense is easy because there are features undesirable about this man Jesus. He claimed to be God among us, and he demands everything from us.

In Jesus' day many people stumbled over what they knew about his personal background—and it takes real greatness not to be offended at those whom we know well. Many also stumbled when, with confidence in him at its peak, he disillusioned them by talking of humility and suffering.

He offended because he had no official status; because he called for a revision of the idea and practice of goodness; because of his unorthodoxy, so stubbornly persisted in; because he refused to abide by the recognized limits. He offended because he claimed to forgive.

He asked for sacrifice and humility, virtues that He demonstrated personally—to the lengths of death by crucifixion. He offended by the very demonstration of what sacrifice meant, the cross. He was so "weak"! He called for such a change, such a price!

But suppose he was the Christ? God the Son?

The offense has never ceased.

Blessed is he who is not offended.

Faith takes up its cross and follows.

John the Baptist, languishing in prison, had sent two friends to interview Jesus. John wanted a word of assurance that he whose way he had prepared was indeed the Expected One. Where there was question and doubt, the drive for certainty was overpowering. So John looked for security in his disciples' report of their encounter with Jesus. They went and watched, and having seen through the day what Jesus did, they returned to their master with Jesus' words ringing in their ears: Go and commend faith to him. Go and witness to John. " 'Blessed is he who takes no offense at me' " (Matthew 11:6).

In fact, with reference to Jesus, only two possibilities are open to anyone—only two: offense or faith. Jesus did indeed perform many wonderful works, but for some people these miracles never pointed beyond themselves to the Person from whom they issued. They viewed these miracles as merely wonders and not as signs of the inbreaking into human history of the kingdom of God. We could say something similar concerning the prophecies. They could be turned against Jesus, as well as toward him. Was he not rejected by a people nurtured by the Prophetic Word? There was always the possibility of offense. And the greater the extent of the knowledge, the broader the base for offense. The certainty of faith with reference to Jesus comes when one has passed the possibility of offense.

But why should offense have been possible? The fact is that offense was easy because, in spite of the extraordinary features and works that accompanied Jesus, there were undesirable things that made the offense almost a matter of course. In addition, one had to reckon with Jesus' unusual claims and with the strange appeal that surrounded offense with guilt. His demand for faith was a demand for everything. But it was based upon his claim to be God among us. Faith demanded all, yet that claim could be rejected without further ado. "After all, it is hard to take—that this man should be God among us. For indeed we know too much about him! What we know is undesirable. He is such an ordinary man—a man not to be desired, and so to be rejected."

"And coming to his own country he taught them in their synagogue, so that they were astonished, and said, 'Where did this man get this wisdom and these mighty works? Is not this the carpenter's son? Is not his mother called Mary? And are not his brothers James and Joseph and Simon and Judas? And are not all his sisters with us? Where then did this man get all this?' And they took offense at him. But Jesus said to them, 'A prophet is not without honor except in his own country and in his own house' " (chapter 13:54-57).

Those who had watched Jesus grow up admitted his wisdom and his mighty works. They could not help admitting them. However, they stumbled over what they knew about his personal background. It was not possible, they thought, that someone whose parents were so ordinary—the father a worker with wood—should have such authority over them. It was not possible, thought the priest and the teacher, that the authority of someone like Jesus should rival theirs.

They had known him from childhood. They were his elders, after all, and really responsible for what he had now become. He was even now just turning 30, and such a promising young man! If only he would listen to their words and conform to their pattern! He must not go his own way, although too much evidence indicated that he was. But his teachings, so simple and yet so demanding—yes, there was the rub! "Shall I hear what God is saying through him to me, through the miracles and signs? Or shall I look at him as merely the joiner's hand, the stripling on Nazareth's streets, the son of a good, devoted common laborer?" "And the choice goes by forever 'Twixt that darkness and that light." [27]

It takes the greatness of humility not to be offended at the lives, words, accomplishments, and witness of those we know well. "That this boy, just yesterday learning to walk, then to carry the planks and to ride the ass, until now a familiar figure along with other lads around the village well—that he should tell us what God's will is!" The paradox and the humiliation of it!

He was easy to reject. But faith was another matter.

Something like the reverse of this took place too. You did not know him. One day you saw his miracles, and immediately you admired the strength and character of this most courageous man. Then, and that was the letdown, when your admiration for him and your confidence in him were at their peak, he would throw a wet blanket over it all by saying strange things about his kingdom, humility, and suffering. Now you had to decide. And thus came the conflict and the doubt, the possibility of offense—or the rebuilding of faith. "Then it is the brave man chooses, while the coward stands aside." [28]

We ourselves find it hard to treat all people alike. The same idea suggested by different people may produce opposite responses. We find it humiliating to accept ideas from some individuals and gratifying to accept the same ideas from others. Truth or error is often accepted or rejected because of an attitude to the person who brings it rather than for its own sake.

Now, Jesus had no official status. He had no office. He had no official authority. He was what we would call a free lance. He just spoke truth. He just appeared among humanity. In many respects he was just an ordinary man. He was such an ordinary person that the fact that God was among mankind in him could be most easily missed.

"He comes to us as one unknown." [29] That is it. God comes to us incognito, and we can easily miss His presence. We can miss the divine in the human. We must always beware lest in passing by the ordinary, we pass God by. He has "no beauty that we should desire him" (Isaiah 53:2). He may offend. The possibility of offense is always present. It may easily pass into actual offense.

He is a good man. Of that there is no question. Yet he calls for such a revision of the idea of goodness that it almost turns the mind. If he only would revise his idea of goodness, he would be acceptable. But he refuses, and so he leaves us with the decision to be offended or to believe. Of all decisions, that is the most difficult—and the most crucial.

He is so wise a man, so fearless a preacher, and so penetrating an analyst of the religious situation! But "unfortunately" he is unorthodox, and as everyone knows, we must preserve orthodoxy at all costs. So we try to correct him. But there is no correction forthcoming—except that of ourselves. Although it is humiliating, we know all the while that he is right and that we with our vaunted pride in a dead creed are wrong. And always he asks us to follow him, in some way or other. We could deny the demand, but we could never fail to recognize it.

He does such wonders and miracles! That is indeed fine. But he refuses to recognize the agreed-on limits and barriers, and that is too much to take. The problem is that he will not remain quiet about his "preposterous" views concerning human sin and divine grace. It is hard enough to hear him talk about the radicalness of human sin and the absoluteness of God's grace. But he goes even further and claims to be the instrument of that grace, the vehicle of that forgiveness. Such claims compound the preposterousness of it all. Shall one believe or shall one stumble? Offense or faith? To be offended is so easy!

The two ways of responding to Jesus are clearly portrayed in the story of the healing of the man born blind. "They said to him, 'What did he do to you? How did he open your eyes?' He answered them, 'I have told you already, and you would not listen. Why do you want to hear it again? Do you too want to become his disciples?' And they reviled him, saying, 'You are his disciple, but we are disciples of Moses. We know that God has spoken to Moses, but as for this man, we do not know where he comes from.' The man answered, 'Why, this is a marvel! You do not know where he comes from, and yet he opened my eyes. We know that God does not listen to sinners, but if any one is a worshiper of God and does his will, God listens to him. Never since the world began has it been heard that any one opened the eyes of a man born blind. If this man were not from God, he could do nothing.' They answered him, 'You were born in utter sin, and you would teach us?' And they cast him out.

"Jesus heard that they had cast him out, and having found him he said, 'Do you believe in the Son of man?' He answered, 'And who is he, sir, that I may believe in him?' Jesus said to him, 'You have seen him, and it is he who speaks to you.' He said, 'Lord, I believe'; and he worshiped him" (John 9:26-38).

There it is—the contrast as stark as it has ever been. The issue was over the definition of sin and grace. " 'How can a man who is a sinner do such signs?' " (verse 16). " 'We know that God does not listen to sinners' " (verse 31). Sinner or—could it be?—he was God himself among us. Faith or offense! The possibility of offense was most real, as was the possibility of faith. The light was shining in the darkness, but the darkness neither understood nor overcame that light (see chapter 1:5). With light comes the possibility of offense, and with offense at the light comes judgment. That judgment issues from the same Source as the light. Darkness follows the day, so we should appreciate the light while it is present. If one stumbles—that is, if one is offended in the light—he is already in darkness (chapter 11:9).

The chips were down. To be confronted with Jesus' claims was enough. To be confronted with the claims of Jesus through a man born blind and " 'born in . . . sin' " was more than enough. The possibility of offense turned into actual offense. "And they cast him out." Him—the blind man; but also him—the healer of the blind, the bearer of light, the light himself.

The chips were down, too, during his last hours. His lowliness became manifest in all its fullness. The humiliation was pressed to its bitter end—the cross. Judas betrayed him. They all forsook him and fled. Later Peter and John followed afar off. Peter denied him. Was this the Christ? Was this the kind of Christ for which they had been waiting? That he who had such powers should let it come to this! There must have been some other way! So it was that Jesus' own disciples passed from the possibility of offense to *actual* offense.

The offense has never been removed from the gospel. There will always remain the occasion for stumbling. "But if I, brethren, still preach circumcision, why am I still persecuted? In that case the stumbling block of the cross has been removed" (Galatians 5:11). Jesus demanded total obedience. Paul preached that same demand. Jesus' claims were total and all-inclusive. For Paul it was not "Jesus and. . ." but "Jesus only!" One could not rely upon any deed or capacity for acceptance with God. Jesus only—not Jesus and works, Jesus and circumcision, Jesus and anything. The demand remains the same. They rejected Him. They will reject his followers. " 'If they do this when the wood is green, what will happen when it is dry?' " (Luke 23:31).

The offense at the Lord will be directed against those who repeat his demand. Every genuine ministry will provide the occasion for offense (as it also provides the occasion for faith). Then the minister has new cause for offense, for he can take offense when others take offense at Jesus Christ. Furthermore, offense against the representatives of Christ may come from unexpected sources, for which we may not always be prepared. When the minister or the witness is offended at another's offense at him, it means that he has become offended at Jesus, for we are his ministers. We are to endure offense but never to be offended. Rather, through it all we are to commend with persistence our Lord and Master. To identify oneself with the gospel of Jesus Christ is to become a cause of offense.

A few years ago a piece of writing appeared with the title "Should Such a Faith Offend?" The answer is that where there is a genuine appeal for real faith the possibility of offense is present. It is simply naive and unrealistic to think that people will not hurt us because we believe. "They would not harm me because I am a Christian, would they?" Only ignorance of church history makes such a question possible. They will. They will reject. Along with the Christ whom they reject will be those who bear witness to that Christ. When people choose offense rather than faith, the believer occasions further offense.

But what of ourselves? Jesus' weakness and manhood offend us. We are quite ready to put ourselves on the side of a God who moves in with thunder and lightning, storm, fire, and sword. If the call were for soldiers to fight for such a God, there would be no difficulty. But instead He calls us to be disciples who give up all. Our God comes in weakness and asks us to share it.

Then there is the cost involved. To make the change means that the whole of existence becomes precarious. And for what? For the first disciples it meant never to know where they would sleep; to be always hounded by the parsons and the bishops; then, to climax it all, to become independent sufferers for his sake. It was clearly a costly choice. It still is. In different walks of life he, the humble one, makes the same unrelenting demand.

But suppose the Humble One was God the Son? Suppose this man was God in the flesh? Suppose God chose to come to His creation in that way? To be offended at him would then be to reject God. To reject the Humble One and the humiliation would be to reject Omnipotence. To turn from him would be to turn from that to which the prophets had looked. It brings us to the brink of decision. Is this how God speaks to mankind? The possibility of offense exists just as long as there is the choice for faith.

" 'Blessed is he who takes no offense at me.' " It seems so paradoxical! Blessed are those who are willing to lose all. Blessed are those who are rejected, criticized, and ostracized. If that state is blessed, faith is, indeed, the rarest of gifts. To those for whom the possibility of offense or faith has issued in faith, there is no talk of sacrifice, but only of joy and thanksgiving. We manifest no pride in what we have denied ourselves, simply because we have no consciousness of having denied ourselves anything. " 'Let him who boasts, boast of the Lord' " (1 Corinthians 1:31).

But the Lord of glory is the crucified Lord, the Lord unknown—incognito—to the individual of the world. Such people "crucified the Lord of glory" (chapter 2:8). The Lord in whom faith glories is the Lord who went to the cross and who reigns from that cross. Faith is a relationship with the God who went to the cross. Faith takes up its cross and follows, joyfully and thankfully. "But far be it from me to glory except in the cross of our Lord Jesus Christ" (Galatians 6:14).

" 'Blessed is he who takes no offense at me.' "

Questions

1. Why were the unbelieving offended at Jesus?
2. Is there still cause for offense at him? Specify.
3. Offense or faith. Is there a third alternative? Explain.

Chapter 14

Expectation and Faith

Where there is expectation there is trust. Faith is the basis of hope. Faith creates the atmosphere in which expectation has meaning, even when the wish is denied. Neither fulfilled nor unfulfilled expectation deceives genuine faith. Faith remains strong through frustrated expectation. When the heart is full of faith, no disappointment can empty it.

Have faith in God, and the future is yours.

Making a wish is easy. There's nothing to it. Even children do it. To wish for someone else is also easy. In fact, nothing is easier. The words slip out; the sentence is spoken. We express the desire, and there the matter may rest. The words expressing the empty wish pass out into the empty air and may fall back unnoticed, for they were never noticed when they were initially spoken.

Nothing is easier than wishing. A wish may be a tinsel streamer glittering for a moment in the borrowed light of a gaudy candle. It may be a strip of ignited magnesium, burning in intensity but leaving little residue. A wish may be a quickly forgotten word, empty for the hearer because it was empty for the speaker. The repetition of a cliché, the dispatch of a formalized product of the printer's art, the stereotyped response to an equally stereotyped advance: that is to wish. To wish with words (how otherwise?) but without the heart is easy.

My wish in closing this book shall be an imperative, and the imperative shall be reminiscent of an old story. Jesus had been teaching on the western shore of Galilee. He was weary. Moreover, he had work to do on the eastern shore. The other side called him. So he turned to his disciples and invited, " 'Let us go across to the other side' " (Mark 4:35). Mark recounts the dismissal of the multitude; Jesus' entry into the ship with his disciples; the boarding of other little ships by some of the crowd; the tremendous storm; the request made of Jesus, who had been sleeping; the word that stilled the tempest; the arrival on the other shore; and the story of the stilling of another tempest there.

Life is a series of voyages to the other side. The Master calls, with a meaning suited to the experiences of each one, "Let us pass over unto the other side" (verse 35, K.J.V.). The call comes to each: to service; to embrace some new duty hitherto unknown; to overcome some temptation, as that ancient tempest needed overcoming; to encounter some new and unexpected hazard or happiness. "Let us pass over."

The storm arose on the way across. While it raged, the Master slept. How often we encounter similar storms in life. Often it appears that it is easier to stop than not to have started. To start is easy; to keep going—that is the test. For storms arise on the way across. Our intention may be excellent, our desire sincerely expressed, but to face the storm needs more than intention and desire.

Wish has to do with expectation. It has to do, through the future, with the present and with the past. While we may say that we live the present into the future, we may perhaps better say that we live the future into the present. Expectation of what may be is either fulfilled or disappointed. Thus one cannot live out of such expectation alone. Expectations disappointed turn bitter with a bitterness that embitters the present and the past. Christian believers have no genuine expectation apart from trust. There is no future if there is no commitment. Where there is no faith there is no hope, for faith is the basis of hope.

Thus, for believers the fulfillment of this or that expectation (desire, ambition, wish; call it what you will) is not the all-important matter. Nor, indeed, is the lack of such fulfillment. There are expectations, and there is faith. The future happiness of believers does not depend upon a series of fulfilled wishes. Nor, on the other hand, is unhappiness the inevitable outcome when first one and then another wish remains unfulfilled. Believers learn to be content in every state. Does an unexpected event negate our desire in this matter or that? What of it? If we possess only expectation and no genuine faith, the negation of our wish may destroy us. But if we have genuine faith, this or that expectation is shaped by our faith and fulfilled in that faith, be the expectation itself fulfilled or denied. Faith creates the atmosphere in which expectation has meaning. It does not, however, produce the expectation of signs and wonders, without which one finds—like the Biblical skeptics—he cannot believe. A faith that rests upon signs and wonders of any kind is not faith. Faith can look on tempests and is never shaken. It can sleep in the storms on the way across.

Thus, as Christians, we do not wish that this or that expectation shall be fulfilled. Our wish goes deeper than that. We wish for a faith that can survive unfulfilled expectations. We wish for a faith that can ride the tempests and expect to arrive at the haven. We wish for a faith that is fulfilled in our true end. It will not be deceived by fulfilled expectations. We wish for the future of faith; the present that is futured in faith; the future that is presented in faith.

I bid you faith: the faith which takes the disappointed expectation and shapes that new and unexpected ingredient into a better person; the faith that can smile in the midst of prosperity, because it is undeceived by it; the faith that, because God gives it and it is directed to Him, can see the fleeting scenes of human life under the eye of eternity.

But "we so often fall into error because we look for an assurance of our expectation, instead of an assurance of faith that we believe."[30] We can find ourselves truly nowhere else than in God. We can find ourselves by no other means than by faith. And faith may rebuke the expectation. Although the expectation may be disappointed, faith is assured because God gives it. It requires no assurance other than its subsistence. Expectation may be frustrated, disappointed, and shattered; but faith may be engendered, fulfilled, and edified through the frustration, disappointment, and shattering of the dreamed-of-expectation. If we fill our heart only with expectation, we may well render it empty. But when we are full of faith, our heart is always filled. No sorrow or pain lies beyond the compass of faith—neither the great tragedy nor the peccadillo.

I bid you faith. Not in this or that object of your desire, even if it be a religious desire, for the deepest sin may be lurking just there. Believe in God. Believe God. Have faith. With faith the future is yours, because the present is yours.

"Let us pass over unto the other side." That is an appropriate word for us. It is both exhortation and a promise. The Master calls us to faith—a faith that will hold through the storms on the way across. It is the kind of faith Jesus had. Through wind and water it can repose in the peace that vanquishes anxiety, the stillness that knows no fear.

Questions

1. Is disappointed or fulfilled expectation a barrier to faith?
2. Specify the distinction between expectation and faith.

Epilogue

What I now wish to say I originally intended to include as the latter half of the introduction. I think you will see that there is good reason for putting it here. I wanted to say something about the *form* of this book. It is a series of chapters united by a common theme. Most of these chapters represent addresses given verbally. If this book had been a theological treatise, I would have worked out in more detail the implications of some of the positions taken here. For example, one would need to examine in greater depth and in terms of a whole range of relationships the meaning of faith. Two questions would then be significant: How is faith related to knowledge and to experience? How, if at all, does faith depend upon history?

At times in our personal experience some ideas make a lasting impression on us. We find joy in them, the joy of a new discovery. So too is it in the experience of a community. If one says only what one has said before, experience becomes static. If the community hears only what it has always heard, it loses its vitality and its joy. These themes—perhaps I should say, "this theme"—marked a beginning for me. I must stress that—*a beginning.* I have seen them also do the same for other Christians. I found myself believing. I discovered that I had faith.

I found also that I could not take that faith for granted. We all, in the midst of our fallen human experience, know what it is to fail to exercise faith at important times, to fail to relate it to the rest of our human experience. We know what it is to have faith questioned and to question it ourselves. And then we know, sometimes in spite of our past, how we confess that faith again. We hear and consider the objections made to the claims of Christian faith.

We glimpse something of the possibilities of such faith for the interpretation of our experience of the world in which we live. We have to think about and take an attitude to teachings that we formerly accepted without question. The maintaining of faith, like the interpretation of faith, is thus a quest—a quest that is also a gift and an answer. It is something that we, as individuals and as a community, get, as well as something we do. It is gift, and it is task. To say anything less is to do it injustice.

"Justification by faith" is a theological principle. It receives its classical expression in Paul. It takes a different form in Augustine. And once again it is renewed and reapplied in Luther. In each case its meaning is different. Its expression today will be different again. If it is a fruitful principle, it will have applications for us in our particular time, and also in times to come.

Of course, justification by faith can become a slogan, like many another. It is possible to focus upon *one* of the terms of the slogan, and then it will mean something rather different than if another of the terms is emphasized. Perhaps by talking about righteousness—justification—we may discover the meaning of faith. We could gain a great deal of help from contemporary theological writers on this issue.

For example, the principle of justification by faith can be related to the question about knowledge of God. If we are justified by faith and not by knowledge, then what must we know so as to be justified, so as to have faith? How can we believe in a God whom we do not know? How can we have faith unless we grasp the knowledge that God is love, for example? What shall we say of the revelation of God? Of the historical Jesus—how much do you have to know about Jesus to believe that God reveals Himself in him? Much? Little? What about our knowledge of the world, nature, and society? Start with faith, and the whole spectrum of theology appears.

"Justification by faith" has its own history. What I must stress is that it is *one* form of expressing the Christian message. It is one particular theological idiom. Sometimes the historical and social context (and that includes the ecclesiastical situation) makes a particular idiom relevant at a given place at a given time. But that does *not* mean that the particular principle, in this case that of justification by faith, is the only idiom, the most important idiom, or the best. It cannot say all that has to be said about Christianity.

I have not intended to engage in controversy or polemics. I do not believe that we spend our time most profitably deploying the concepts that have now become historical, the concepts used in the debate between Augustine and Pelagius, or in the latter discussion—what has come to be called the Arminian controversy. These debates teach us that if we define the key concepts as they did, there are a limited number of possibilities in which they can be related together.

What happens in some Christian circles is that the debate about grace, faith, law, works, and justification is continued today in much the same way as it was in days gone by. So the same alternative positions emerge as emerged in the older controversy. Orthodox and heterodox positions can be identified as they were so long ago. Of course, it may be exciting to discover something *for ourselves* for the first time. But we should not think that that is the first time such positions have been worked out. A serious consideration of the history of debate on these questions, one must think, is a basic prerequisite for engaging in contemporary discussion about faith. Such consideration will lead us on to other important problems, where perhaps we can make some real discoveries. Unless doctrinal discussion is related to real faith, it becomes sterile, and debate unprofitable.

The terms of the slogan "Justification by Faith" and related terms can be used to communicate important emphases *if* they can be understood. So in a contemporary world we will need to employ contemporary idiom to be most widely effective. Otherwise the Christian community will become unduly introversive. They in their time never did settle the issue decisively. Traditional interpretations and the use of traditional terminology leave questions unanswered. And to many people the terminology itself is strange and restricting. The traditional debates left dilemmas unresolved. Key concepts were insufficiently developed, with the result that within the limits of those debates the issue was not and could not be settled. We do not want to repeat the past. We cannot do so, since we are aware of questions they did not directly consider—questions of nineteenth—and twentieth—century skepticism and agnosticism, for example.

What we can learn from the history of the slogan and its accompanying doctrinal formulations is that it functioned as a corrective: in Paul's day against the Judaizing Christians; in Augustine's time against the Pelagians. (Augustine spoke most emphatically of grace rather than of faith.) It functioned as a corrective for Luther against the traffic in indulgences and a system of penance; by later Lutherans against the dogmatism of Lutheranism; and in evangelical circles against reliance on a system of dogma and ethics as if they were the be-all and end-all.

The previous discussions shared certain concerns in common: an interest in human effort and achievement, a desire to be both positive and negative in the right way and with the right balance, a recognition of God's activity in relation to human response, and a determination that whatever should be said about these shall be true to the deliverances of Christian experience. The emphasis, however, was on the experience of the individual: how, given faith, that faith is possible and how it expresses itself. Little interest in the corporate experience was shown: How is the Christian experience of the community as a community possible? The discussion was conducted in nonhistorical terms. Now it must be discussed in historical and corporate terms. *That* could find a salutary expression in doctrine.

Endnotes

[1] C. Ryder Smith, *The Bible Doctrine of Grace* (London: The Epworth Press, 1956), pp. 56, 57.

[2] Wilhelm Niesel, *The Theology of Calvin,* trans. Harold Knight (Philadelphia: Westminster Press, 1956), p. 124.

[3] *De Natura et Gratia, contra Pelagium,* Chap. IV.

[4] *Institutes,* Book III, Chap. xi, Par. VII.

[5] Francis Thompson, "The Hound of Heaven."

[6] William Cowper, from the hymn, "God Moves in a Mysterious Way."

[7] Edmond Jacob, *Theology of the Old Testament,* trans. by Arthur W. Heathcote and Philip J. Allcock (New York: Harper & Brothers, 1958), p. 227.

[8] Eusebius, *The Ecclesiastical History,* Book V, Chap. i, Sec. 19, in Loeb Classical Library, *Eusebius,* vol. 1, p. 415.

[9] *The Martyrdom of Polycarp,* Chap. IX, Sec. 3, in Loeb Classical Library, *The Apostolic Fathers,* vol. 2, p. 325.

[10] Ellen G. White, *Life Sketches* (Mountain View, Calif.: Pacific Press Pub. Assn., 1915), p. 196.

[11] Martin Luther, from the hymn, "A Mighty Fortress Is Our God."

[12] Cowper, *loc. cit.*

[13] Dietrich Bonhoeffer, *Creation and Fall,* trans. John C. Fletcher (London: SCM Press, Ltd., 1962), p. 16.

[14] Martin Luther, *Lectures on Romans,* trans. and ed. Wilhelm Pauck, in The Library of Christian Classics. (Philadelphia: Westminster Press, 1961), Vol. XV, p. 127.

[15] C. Ryder Smith, *The Bible Doctrine of Man* (London: The Epworth Press,1951), p. 191.

[16] "On Translating: An Open Letter," *Works of Martin Luther,* Vol. V, pp. 15-22.

[17] Gerhard Ebeling, *The Nature of Faith,* trans. by Ronald G. Smith (Philadelphia: Fortress Press, 1961), p. 34.

[18] Smith, *The Bible Doctrine of Man,* pp. 248, 249.

[19] *Ibid.,* p. 191.

[20] Luther, *Lectures on Romans,* p. 125.

[21] Dietrich Bonhoeffer, *The Cost of Discipleship,* trans. R. H. Fuller (New York: The Macmillan Company, 1963), p. 69.

[22] J. S. Whale, *The Protestant Tradition* (London: Cambridge University Press, 1955), p. 67.

[23] H. R. Mackintosh, *The Christian Experience of Forgiveness* (London: James Nisbet and Company, Ltd., 1947), p. 242.

[24] Bernard of Clairvaux, from the hymn "Jesus, the Very Thought of Thee."

[25] John Milton, "On His Blindness."

[26] *"O Deus, ego amo te."* Attributed to Francis Xavier (1506-1552), trans. Edward Caswell (1814-1878).

[27] James Russell Lowell, from the hymn "Once to Every Man and Nation."

[28] *Ibid.*

[29] Albert Schweitzer, *The Quest of the Historical Jesus,* trans. W. Montgomery (London: Adam and Charles Black, 1973), p. 401.

[30] Sören Kierkegaard, *Edifying Discourses,* trans. David F. and Lillian Marvin Swenson and ed. Paul L. Holmer (New York: Harper & Brothers, 1958), p. 26.